Math Logic & Word Problems

1–2

Written by
Vicky Shiotsu

Editors: Carla Hamaguchi and Collene Dobelmann
Illustrator: Jenny Campbell
Designer/Production: Moonhee Pak/Carrie Rickmond
Cover Designer: Barbara Peterson
Art Director: Tom Cochrane
Project Director: Carolea Williams

Table of Contents

Introduction

Each book in the *Power Practice*™ series contains over 100 ready-to-use activity pages to provide students with skill practice. The fun activities can be used to supplement and enhance what you are already teaching in your classroom. Give an activity page to students as independent class work, or send the pages home as homework to reinforce skills taught in class. An answer key is provided for quick reference.

Math Logic & Word Problems 1–2 has been designed specifically to build mathematical knowledge and develop critical thinking skills. The activities in this book include visual puzzles, logic problems, patterning activities, multi-step problems, and more. All of the activities promote creative thinking and give students opportunities to apply a variety of problem solving strategies.

The pages in this book are grouped according to the categories derived from five National Council of Teachers of Mathematics (NCTM) content standards: Number and Operations, Algebra, Geometry, Measurement, and Data Analysis and Probability. Each category includes a wide range of formats and skills. In some cases, a progression of skills is presented over several pages to give students practice in solving a particular type of problem.

Use these ready-to-go activities to "recharge" skill review and give students the power to succeed!

Name ______________________ Date ____________

How Many Beads?

Use Objects, Visualize

Anna put a cloth over each string of beads. Read the clues. Write how many beads are under each cloth.

A. There are 7 beads in all.

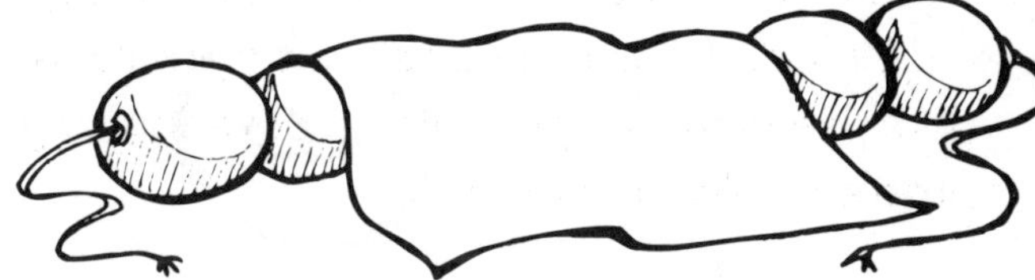

How many beads are under the cloth? _____

B. There are 8 beads in all.

How many beads are under the cloth? _____

C. There are 11 beads in all.

How many beads are under the cloth? _____

D. There are 9 beads in all.

How many beads are under the cloth? _____

E. There are 14 beads in all.

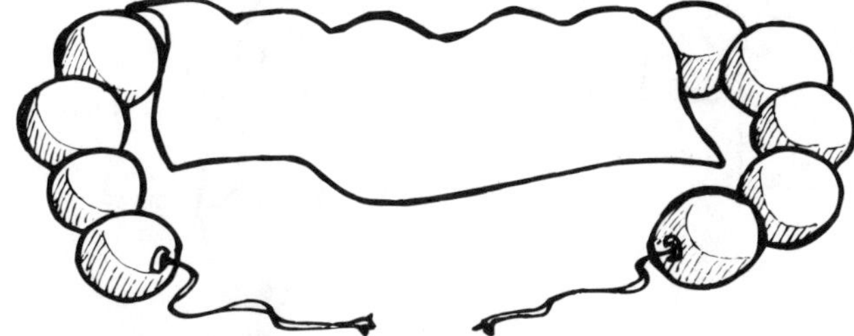

How many beads are under the cloth? _____

F. There are 10 beads in all.

How many beads are under the cloth? _____

Name ______________________________ Date ______________

Super Sums

Organize Information, Guess and Check

Write number sentences that add up to 15. Use the numbers 1 to 9.
Do not use a number more than once in each sentence.

A. ☐ + ☐ + ☐ = 15

B. ☐ + ☐ + ☐ = 15

C. ☐ + ☐ + ☐ = 15

D. ☐ + ☐ + ☐ = 15

Try This! Write number sentences with four numbers that add up to 15.

E. ☐ + ☐ + ☐ + ☐ = 15

F. ☐ + ☐ + ☐ + ☐ = 15

Name ______________________________ Date ______________

Hidden Sums

Guess and Check

Look at the numbers in the box. Circle three numbers in a row that add up to 12. The numbers can go across or down. When you are finished, 12 sets of numbers should be circled. The first one is done for you.

4	5	8	3	2	7	9
6	9	5	1	6	3	2
2	3	3	6	5	3	2
3	5	4	8	2	4	8
8	1	2	9	5	5	6
1	9	5	7	1	4	5

Name ______________________________ Date ______________

Plus and Minus Puzzler

Guess and Check

Look at each row of numbers. Write + or – in the circles to make two number sentences that are equal.

A. 3 (+) 5 = 9 (–) 1

B. 6 ( ) 4 = 8 ( ) 6

C. 10 ( ) 5 = 2 ( ) 3

D. 6 ( ) 6 = 9 ( ) 3

E. 11 ( ) 2 = 3 ( ) 6

F. 7 ( ) 3 = 2 ( ) 8

G. 11 ( ) 4 = 12 ( ) 5

H. 8 ( ) 5 = 7 ( ) 6

I. 5 ( ) 3 = 10 ( ) 2

J. 13 ( ) 5 = 6 ( ) 2

K. 10 ( ) 6 = 12 ( ) 8

L. 12 ( ) 3 = 4 ( ) 5

Write two more problems like the ones on this page.

____

____

Name ________________________________ Date ______________

Plus and Minus Challenge

Guess and Check

Look at each row of numbers. Write + or – in the circles to make two number sentences that are equal.

A. 4 (+) 3 (–) 1 = 5 ( ) 5 ( ) 4

B. 2 ( ) 6 ( ) 1 = 7 ( ) 3 ( ) 1

C. 10 ( ) 2 ( ) 3 = 1 ( ) 2 ( ) 2

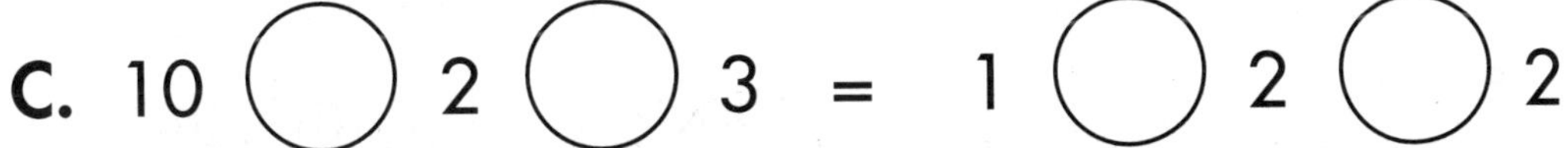

D. 6 ( ) 5 ( ) 3 = 7 ( ) 3 ( ) 2

E. 9 ( ) 2 ( ) 5 = 4 ( ) 4 ( ) 4

F. 3 ( ) 6 ( ) 2 = 8 ( ) 4 ( ) 1

G. 7 ( ) 7 ( ) 5 = 6 ( ) 6 ( ) 3

H. 8 ( ) 3 ( ) 9 = 12 ( ) 4 ( ) 6

I. 13 ( ) 5 ( ) 7 = 5 ( ) 5 ( ) 5

J. 5 ( ) 6 ( ) 4 = 12 ( ) 7 ( ) 2

Name ______________________________ Date ______________

Waiting in Line

Use a Diagram

There are 8 children waiting in line. Look at their picture and solve the problems.

______ ______ ______ ______ ______ ______ ______ ______

A. Cory is second in line. How many children are behind him?

______

B. Dana is fifth in line. How many children are behind her?

______

C. Max is sixth in line. How many children are in front of him?

______

D. Jan is fourth in line. How many children are in front of her?

______

E. Susie is first in line. Brett is seventh in line. How many children are between Susie and Brett? ______

F. Alex is third in line. Lisa is eighth in line. How many children are between Alex and Lisa? ______

G. Write the names of the children under their picture.

Name ______________________ Date ____________

Who Am I?

Logical Thinking

Read the clues. Write the correct name on each line.

Lori

Ricky

Stacy

Evan

Rachel

Max

A. I am older than 10. I am not a girl.

____

B. I am 2 years older than the youngest boy.

____

C. I am 5 years younger than the oldest girl.

____

D. I am older than Lori. I am younger than Evan.

____

E. I am older than Ricky. I am younger than Rachel.

____

F. I am 1 year older than the youngest girl.

____

Name ______________________________ Date ____________

On the Bus

Multi-Step Problems

Solve the problems.

A. There are 6 people on the bus. Then 2 people get off and 1 person gets on. How many people are on the bus now?

B. There are 7 people on the bus. Then 4 people get off and 3 people get on. How many people are on the bus now?

C. There are 10 people on the bus. The bus goes to 3 more stops. At each stop, 2 people get on. No one gets off. How many people are on the bus?

D. There are 15 people on the bus. The bus goes to 2 more stops. At each stop, 4 people get off. How many people are on the bus now?

E. There are 5 people on the bus. Then 6 people get on. At the next stop, some students get on. Now there are 15 people on the bus. How many students got on?

F. There are 12 people on the bus. Then 5 people get off. At the next stop, some boy scouts get on. Now there are 14 people on the bus. How many boy scouts got on?

Name ______________________ Date ____________

Mystery Numbers

Guess and Check

Look at the numbers in each set. Use them to write numbers that match the clues. Do not use a number more than once for each set.

A. The number is even. It is greater than 35. It is less than 50.

5 2 6 3

____

B. The number is odd. It is greater than 85. It is less than 90.

9 8 2 5

____

C. The number is even. It is greater than 60. It is less than 70.

3 7 6 2

____

D. The number is even. It is greater than 60. It is less than 70.

4 6 7 9

____

E. The number is even. It is greater than 25. It is less than 30.

2 8 4 3

____

F. The number is odd. It is greater than 80. It is less than 95.

1 9 7 4

____

G. The number is odd. It is greater than 45. It is less than 75.

3 9 4 2

____

Name ______________________ Date __________

Adding Odd and Even Numbers

Find a Pattern

Add odd and even numbers. Find a pattern.

Even numbers end in 2, 4, 6, 8, and 0.

Odd numbers end in 1, 3, 5, 7, and 9.

A. Add two even numbers together. Is the answer odd or even?

____

$$\begin{array}{r} 12 \\ +6 \\ \hline \end{array} \qquad \begin{array}{r} 24 \\ +32 \\ \hline \end{array} \qquad \begin{array}{r} 40 \\ +18 \\ \hline \end{array}$$

B. Add two odd numbers together. Is the answer odd or even?

____

$$\begin{array}{r} 3 \\ +9 \\ \hline \end{array} \qquad \begin{array}{r} 11 \\ +35 \\ \hline \end{array} \qquad \begin{array}{r} 47 \\ +41 \\ \hline \end{array}$$

C. Add an even number and an odd number together. Is the answer odd or even? ______________________

$$\begin{array}{r} 14 \\ +5 \\ \hline \end{array} \qquad \begin{array}{r} 60 \\ +7 \\ \hline \end{array} \qquad \begin{array}{r} 71 \\ +22 \\ \hline \end{array}$$

D. What happens when you add two even numbers together?

____

E. What happens when you add two odd numbers together?

____

F. What happens when you add an odd number and an even number?

____

Name ______________________ Date ____________

Subtracting Odd and Even Numbers

Find a Pattern

Subtract odd and even numbers.
Find a pattern.

A. Subtract an even number from an even number. Is the answer odd or even?

$$\begin{array}{r} 8 \\ -2 \\ \hline \end{array} \qquad \begin{array}{r} 14 \\ -10 \\ \hline \end{array} \qquad \begin{array}{r} 48 \\ -36 \\ \hline \end{array}$$

____

B. Subtract an odd number from an odd number. Is the answer odd or even?

$$\begin{array}{r} 9 \\ -5 \\ \hline \end{array} \qquad \begin{array}{r} 37 \\ -17 \\ \hline \end{array} \qquad \begin{array}{r} 83 \\ -21 \\ \hline \end{array}$$

____

C. Subtract an even number from an odd number. Subtract an odd number from an even number. Are the answers odd or even?

$$\begin{array}{r} 17 \\ -4 \\ \hline \end{array} \qquad \begin{array}{r} 48 \\ -7 \\ \hline \end{array} \qquad \begin{array}{r} 69 \\ -32 \\ \hline \end{array}$$

____

D. What happens when you subtract an even number from an even number?

____

E. What happens when you subtract an odd number from an odd number?

____

F. What happens when you subtract an even number from an odd number or an odd number from an even number?

____

Name ______________________________ Date ______________

Addition Mysteries

Logical Thinking

Look at each set of numbers. Use the numbers to fill in the boxes. For each problem, use each of the three numbers once.

A.

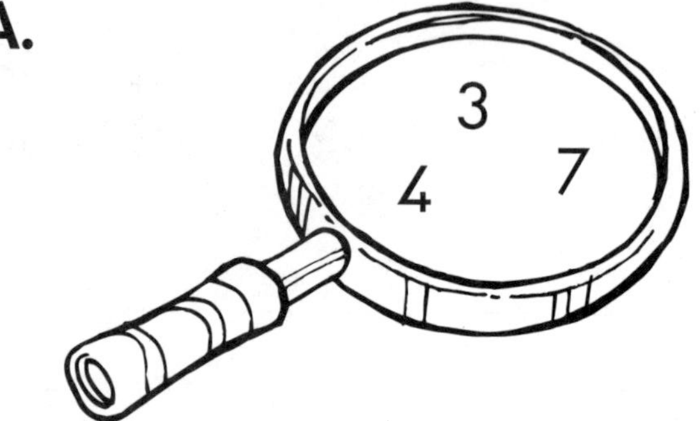


```
  43        1□
+ 14      + □2
----      ----
  57        □9
```

B.

```
  □6        4□
+ 3□      + □7
----      ----
  □7        9□
```

C.

```
  □□        □7
+ 13      + 5□
----      ----
  8□        8□
```

D.

```
  □8        □4
+ □□      + 5□
----      ----
  98        9□
```

Name ______________________________ Date ____________

Subtraction Mysteries

Logical Thinking

Look at each set of numbers. Use the numbers to fill in the boxes. For each problem, use each of the three numbers once.

A.

7 [5] − 3 [2] [4] 3	□ □ − □ 4 3 0

B.

□ □ − 4 1 5 □	8 □ − □ □ 2 2

C.

7 □ − □ 8 6 □	6 □ − □ □ 4 2

D.

□ □ − 1 8 □ 9	9 □ − □ □ 1 8

Name ______________________ Date ____________

Bug Watch

Choose the Operation

Solve the problems.

A. There were 65 bees in a hive. Then 24 bees went out. How many bees were left in the hive?

$$\begin{array}{r} 65 \\ -24 \\ \hline 41 \end{array}$$

___41___ bees

B. There were 30 ants on a log. Then 48 more ants came. How many ants were there altogether?

________ ants

C. Sam saw 21 yellow butterflies. Pam saw 15 orange butterflies. How many butterflies did they see in all?

________ butterflies

D. On Monday, Lynn saw 28 flies. On Tuesday, she saw 11 flies. How many more flies did she see on Monday than on Tuesday?

________ flies

E. There were 54 spotted beetles. There were 45 striped beetles. How many beetles were there in all?

________ beetles

F. There were 36 ladybugs in the yard. Then 31 ladybugs flew away. How many ladybugs were left?

________ ladybugs

G. There were 47 caterpillars on a branch. Then 20 of them crawled away. How many caterpillars were left on the branch?

________ caterpillars

H. There were 41 moths by a tree. There were 27 moths by a pond. How many moths were there in all?

________ moths

Name ______________________________ Date ______________

Sticker Fun

Multi-Step Problems

Solve the problems. You will need to use more than one step for each problem.

A. Cory had some car stickers. He bought 6 more car stickers. Then Cory's friend gave him 3 more car stickers. Now Cory has 49 car stickers in all. How many car stickers did he have at first?

________ car stickers

B. Mindy had 50 dog stickers. She got 5 dog stickers from Dawn and 15 dog stickers from Jay. How many stickers does Mindy have now?

________ dog stickers

C. Emily had 67 silver stars. She gave 12 stars to Sue and some stars to Jan. Now Emily has 47 silver stars left. How many silver stars did Emily give to Jan?

________ silver stars

D. Joe has 18 gold stars. Moe has 6 more gold stars than Joe. How many gold stars do they have altogether?

________ gold stars

Name ______________________ Date ______________

Guess Benny's Number

Logical Thinking

Benny is thinking of a number.
Read the clues to find out what it is.
As you read each clue, cross off the numbers on the chart.
At the end, you will be left with Benny's number.

- The number has two digits.
- Both digits are greater than or equal to 5.
- The tens digit is greater than the ones digit.
- The sum of the digits is 12.

Benny's number is __________.

1	2	3	4	5	6	7	8	9	10
11	12	13	14	15	16	17	18	19	20
21	22	23	24	25	26	27	28	29	30
31	32	33	34	35	36	37	38	39	40
41	42	43	44	45	46	47	48	49	50
51	52	53	54	55	56	57	58	59	60
61	62	63	64	65	66	67	68	69	70
71	72	73	74	75	76	77	78	79	80
81	82	83	84	85	86	87	88	89	90
91	92	93	94	95	96	97	98	99	100

Name ______________________________ Date ______________

Guess Jenny's Number

Logical Thinking

Jenny is thinking of a number.
Read the clues to find out what it is.
As you read each clue, cross off the numbers on the chart.
At the end, you will be left with Jenny's number.

- The number has two digits.
- Both digits are less than 8.
- The ones digit is greater than the tens digit.
- The sum of the digits is 10.
- The number is even.

Jenny's number is __________.

1	2	3	4	5	6	7	8	9	10
11	12	13	14	15	16	17	18	19	20
21	22	23	24	25	26	27	28	29	30
31	32	33	34	35	36	37	38	39	40
41	42	43	44	45	46	47	48	49	50
51	52	53	54	55	56	57	58	59	60
61	62	63	64	65	66	67	68	69	70
71	72	73	74	75	76	77	78	79	80
81	82	83	84	85	86	87	88	89	90
91	92	93	94	95	96	97	98	99	100

Name ______________________________ Date ______________

Number Trios

Make a List

Look at each set of numbers. Using each number once, arrange the digits on each set of cards to make 6 three-digit numbers. The first one is started for you.

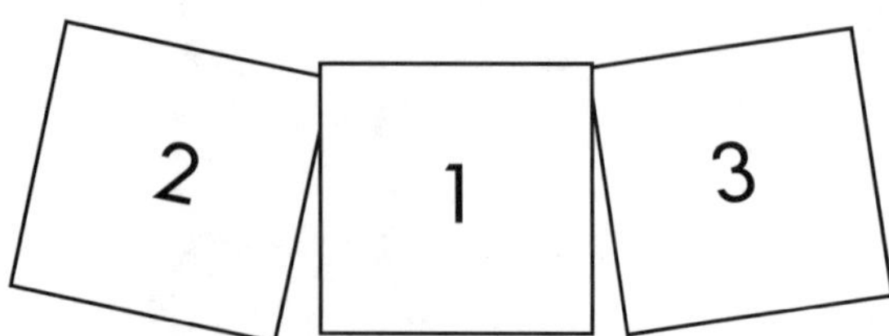

213 ______ 231 ______ 123 ______

______ ______ ______

Write the three digit numbers in order from the smallest to the largest.

A. ______, ______, ______, ______, ______, ______

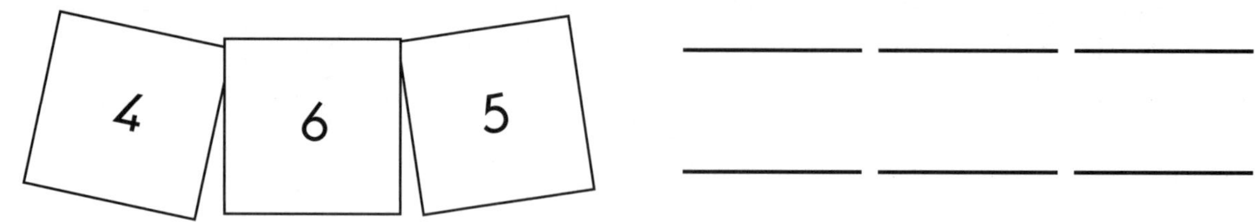

Write the three digit numbers in order from the smallest to the largest.

B. ______, ______, ______, ______, ______, ______

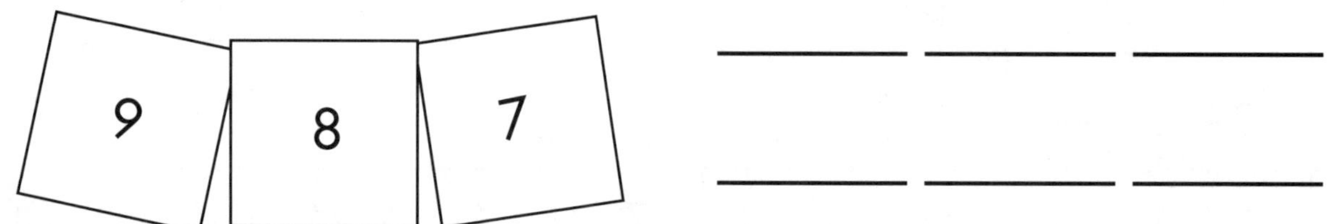

Write the three digit numbers in order from the smallest to the largest.

C. ______, ______, ______, ______, ______, ______

Name ______________________________ Date ______________

Hocus, Pocus!

Logical Thinking

Help the wizard make three-digit numbers.
Use the digits on each set of stars to write each number.

A.

largest three-digit number ____________

smallest three-digit number ____________

largest three-digit number with the 9 in the tens place ______

B.

largest three-digit number ____________

smallest three-digit number ____________

largest three-digit number with the 6 in the ones place ____________

C.

largest three-digit number ____________

smallest three-digit number ____________

largest three-digit number with the 7 in the ones place ____________

Name ______________________________ Date ______________

Book Talk

Multi-Step Problems

Solve the problems. You will need to use more than one step to solve each problem.

A. Emma's job is to put books away at the library.
On Monday she put away 50 books.
On Tuesday she put away 12 more books than on Monday.
How many books did she put away in all?
________ books

B. Brad's book has 150 pages.
On Saturday he read 45 pages.
On Sunday, he read 35 pages.
How many pages does Brad have left to read?
________ pages

C. Kris has 24 books.
Cam has 19 more books than Kris.
Kelly has 5 fewer books than Cam.
How many books do the children have in all?
________ books

D. Lauren has 16 books in her book bag.
Alyssa has half as many books as Lauren.
Kristen has half as many books as Alyssa.
How many books do the children have altogether?
________ books

Name ______________________________ Date ______________

Fun at the Fair

Choose the Operation

Solve the problems.

A. On Saturday, 320 people rode the roller coaster. On Sunday, 425 rode the roller coaster. How many people rode the roller coaster on the weekend? __________ people

B. Cleo the Clown had 270 balloons. She gave 150 away to children. How many balloons did Cleo have left?

__________ balloons

C. There were 100 teddy bears for sale at the fair. By 5:00, there were only 29 teddy bears left. How many teddy bears had been sold?

_________ teddy bears

D. The popcorn seller had 175 bags of popcorn. He sold 96 bags by noon. How many bags of popcorn were left?

_________ bags of popcorn

E. There were 39 apple pies, 14 cherry pies, and 48 pumpkin pies in the baking contest. How many pies were in the contest?

_________ pies

F. There were 190 people eating hot dogs. Half of them put ketchup on their hot dogs. How many did not put ketchup on their hot dogs?

_____ people

G. There were 184 people waiting to get on the Ferris wheel. Then 36 of them got on. How many people were still waiting in line?

_________ people

Name ______________________ Date ____________

Making Cents

Draw a Diagram

Percy Pig has shown you one way you can make 50 cents.

Draw coins to show five other ways you can make 50 cents.

1.

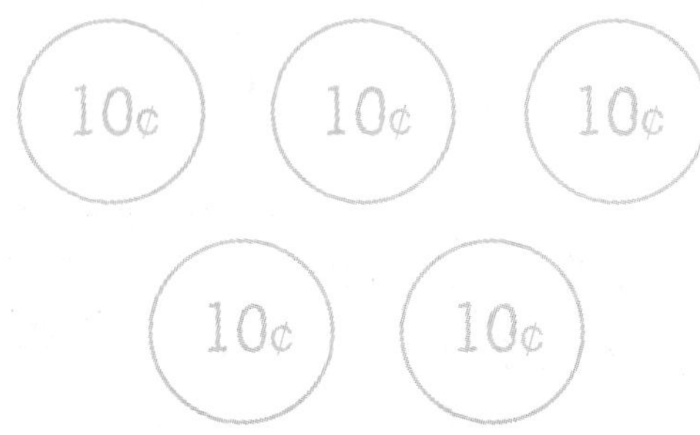

2.

3.

4.

5.

6.

Name ______________________ Date ____________

What's in the Bag?

Logical Thinking

Draw the coins to show what is in each bag.

A. There are 2 coins. They add up to 15¢.

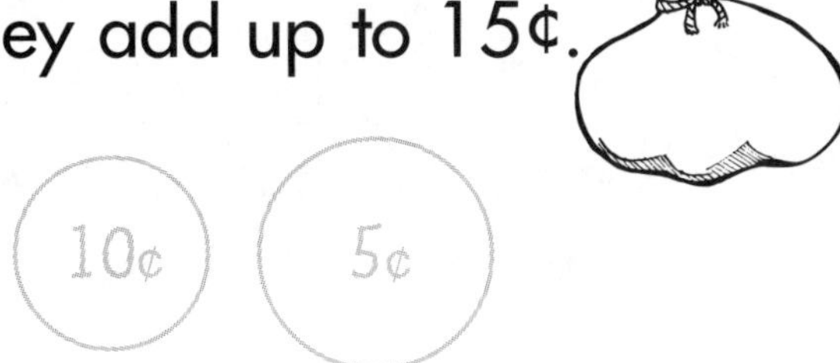

B. There are 2 coins. They add up to 35¢.

C. There are 3 coins. They add up to 45¢.

D. There are 3 coins. They add up to 25¢.

E. There are 3 coins. They add up to 60¢.

F. There are 4 coins. They add up to 60¢.

G. There are 4 coins. They add up to 85¢.

H. There are 5 coins. They add up to 65¢.

Name ______________________ Date ____________

At the Fair

Logical Thinking

Look at the price of each item. Then solve the problems.

25¢
flag

20¢
balloon

50¢
ice cream

75¢
monkey

80¢
clown

A. David has 2 dimes. What can he buy?

____

B. Elsie has 5 dimes. How many flags can she buy?

____

C. Jenna has 2 quarters. What is the most expensive item she can buy?

____

D. Marcus has 3 quarters. What is the most expensive thing he can buy?

____

E. Paul has 2 quarters and 1 dime. How much more money does he need to buy the clown?

____

F. Jessica has 2 quarters and 2 nickels. How much more money does she need to buy the monkey?

____

G. Kim has 3 quarters. How many balloons can she buy?

____

H. Matt has 3 quarters and 2 dimes. He wants to buy 3 different items. What can he buy?

____

Name ______________________________ Date ______________

At the Toy Store

Logical Thinking

Look at the prices of the toys. Then solve the problems.

Top	–	$1.15	Ball	–	$1.25
Car	–	$2.25	Yo-yo	–	$1.00
Bear	–	$3.00	Drum	–	$2.50

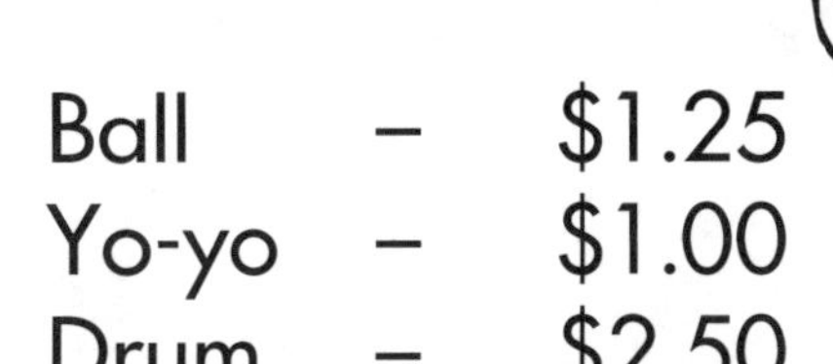

A. Mandy bought two different toys. She spent $4.00. What did she buy?

____

B. Brian bought two different toys. He spent $3.65. What did he buy?

____

C. Sara and Kyle each bought a toy. Sara's toy cost 15¢ more than Kyle's toy. What did each child buy?
Sara ______________ Kyle ______________

D. Nikki and Brandon each bought a toy. Nikki's toy cost $1.00 less than Brandon's toy. What did each child buy?
Nikki ______________ Brandon ______________

E. Scott has $3.00. He will buy two different toys. Which pairs of toys can he buy?

____

Name ______________________ Date ______________

Fun with Pennies and Nickels

Find and Extend a Pattern

Solve each problem.

A. Katie had 10 coins. She started laying them in a pattern like this:

How many cents did Katie have in all? To find out, label the coins below and write the amount.

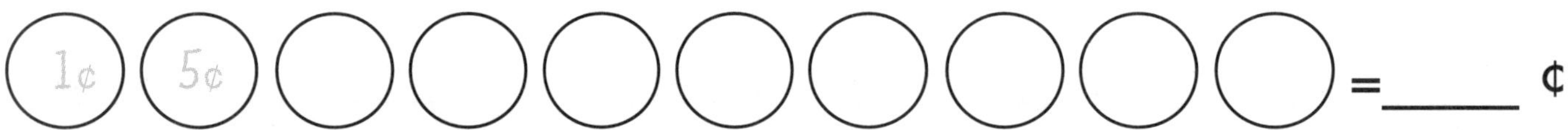

B. Bert had 10 coins. He started laying them in a pattern like this:

How many cents did Bert have in all? To find out, label the coins below and write the amount.

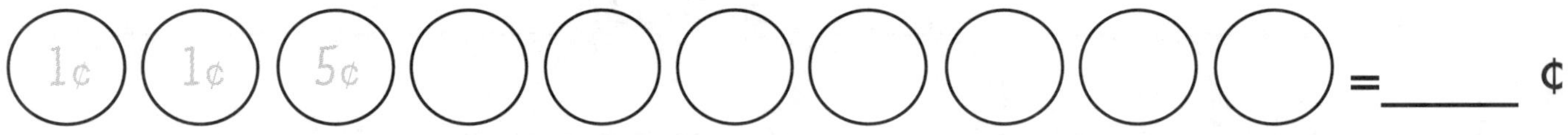

Who had more money—Katie or Bert? ______________________

Name ______________________________ Date ______________

Coin Patterns

Find and Extend a Pattern

Solve each problem.

A. Jake had 10 coins. He started laying them in a pattern like this:

How many cents did Jake have? To find out, label the coins and write the amount.

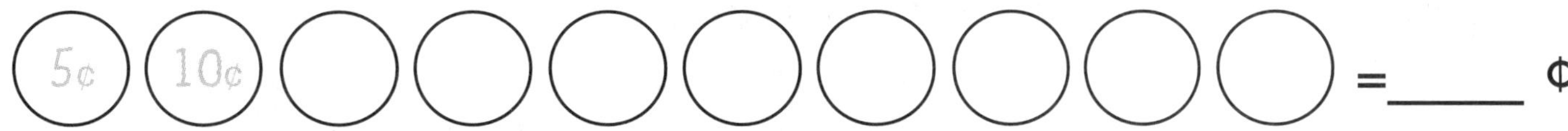

= _____ ¢

B. Kim had 10 coins. She started laying them in a pattern like this:

How many cents did Kim have? To find out, label the coins and write the amount.

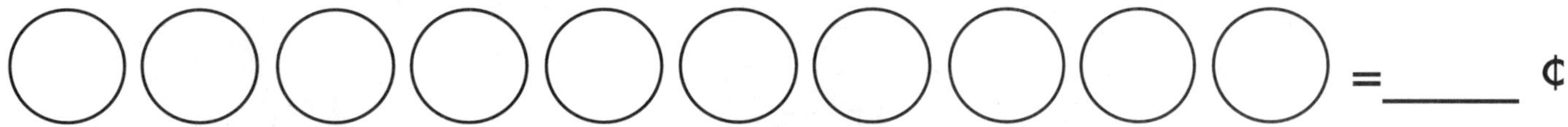

= _____ ¢

C. Julius had 10 coins. He started laying them in a pattern like this:

How many cents did Julius have? To find out, label the coins and write the amount.

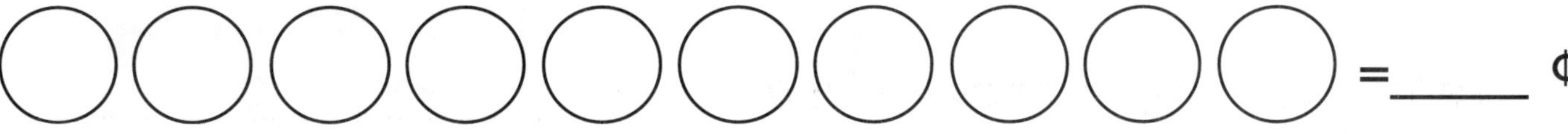

= _____ ¢

Name ______________________________ Date ______________

Find the Fraction

Use a Picture

Two-thirds of the circle is shaded.

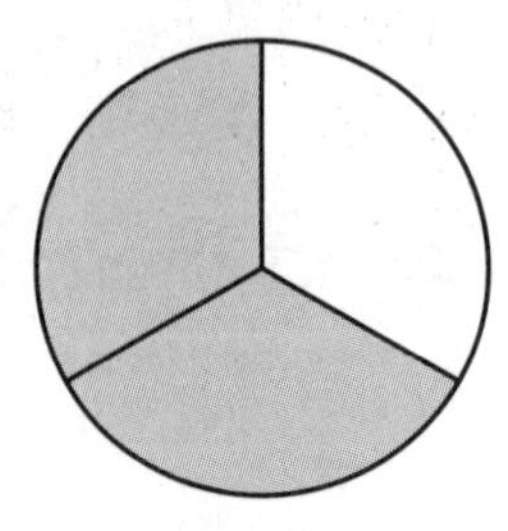

$\frac{2}{3}$

2 — number of parts that are shaded

3 — number of parts in all

Look at each picture. Circle the fraction that tells what part is shaded.

A.

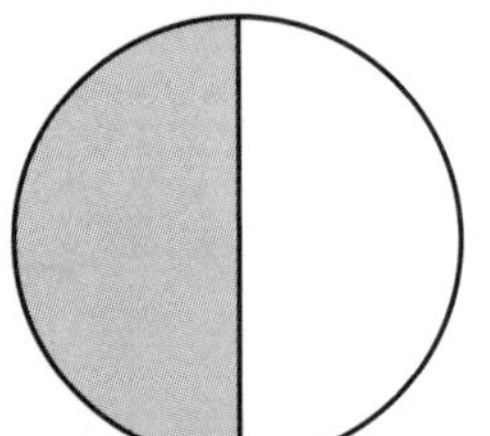

$\frac{1}{2}$ $\frac{2}{1}$ $\frac{2}{3}$

B.

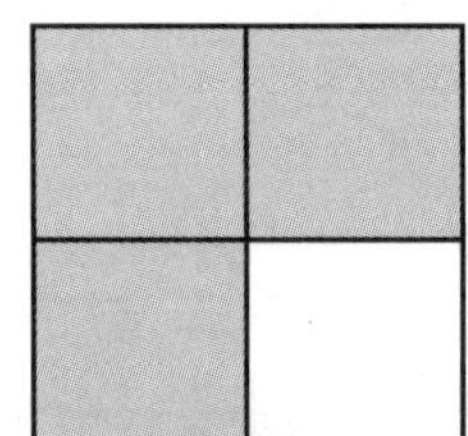

$\frac{4}{4}$ $\frac{3}{4}$ $\frac{2}{4}$

C.

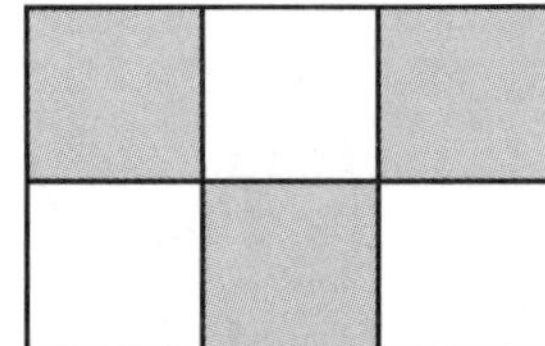

$\frac{1}{6}$ $\frac{5}{6}$ $\frac{3}{6}$

D.

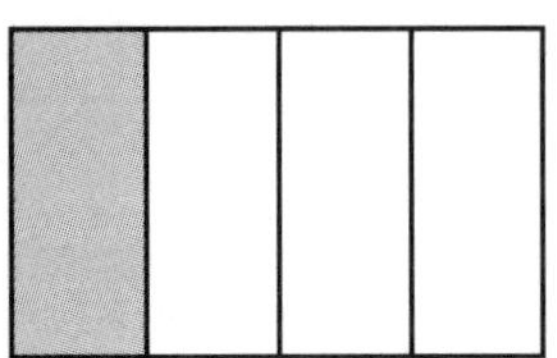

$\frac{1}{4}$ $\frac{1}{3}$ $\frac{2}{3}$

E.

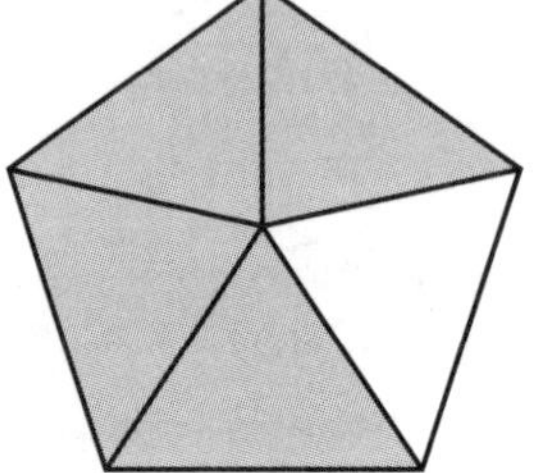

$\frac{3}{5}$ $\frac{1}{4}$ $\frac{4}{5}$

F.

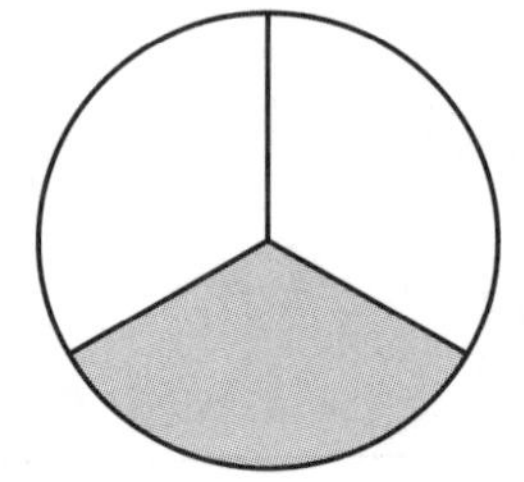

$\frac{1}{2}$ $\frac{1}{3}$ $\frac{1}{4}$

G.

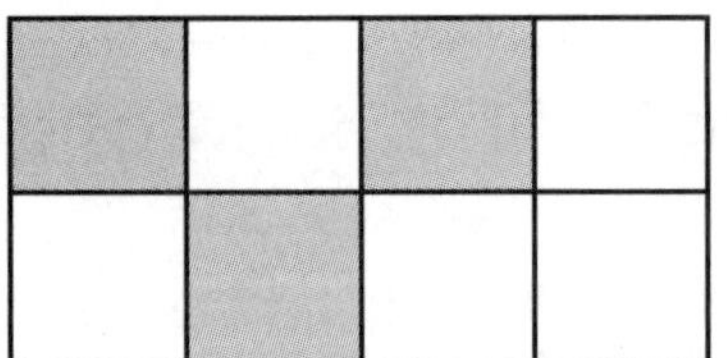

$\frac{3}{5}$ $\frac{3}{8}$ $\frac{6}{8}$

H.

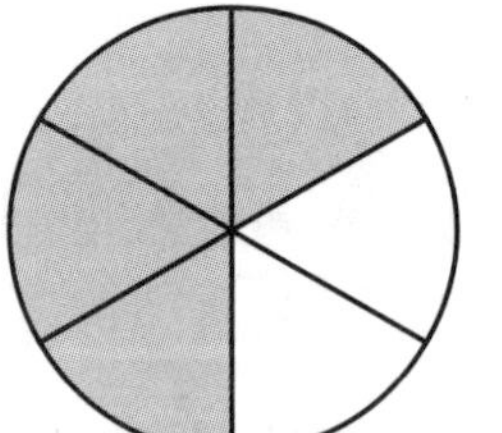

$\frac{2}{4}$ $\frac{1}{3}$ $\frac{4}{6}$

I.

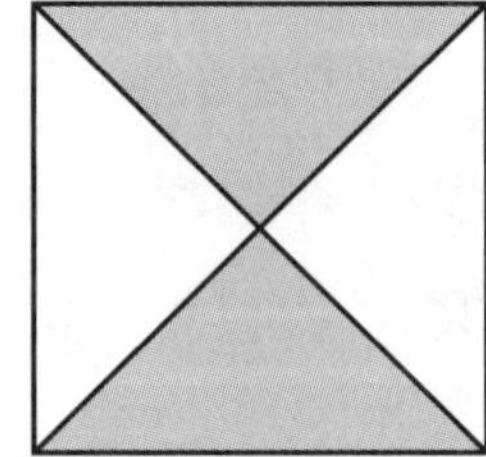

$\frac{2}{4}$ $\frac{2}{2}$ $\frac{3}{4}$

Name ______________________________ Date ______________

Fraction Designs

Visual Thinking

Miss Brown's class folded sheets of paper and then unfolded them. The students colored the parts of the paper to make designs. Read the directions and color the different parts of the paper.

A. Color $\frac{1}{3}$ red.
Color $\frac{2}{3}$ purple.

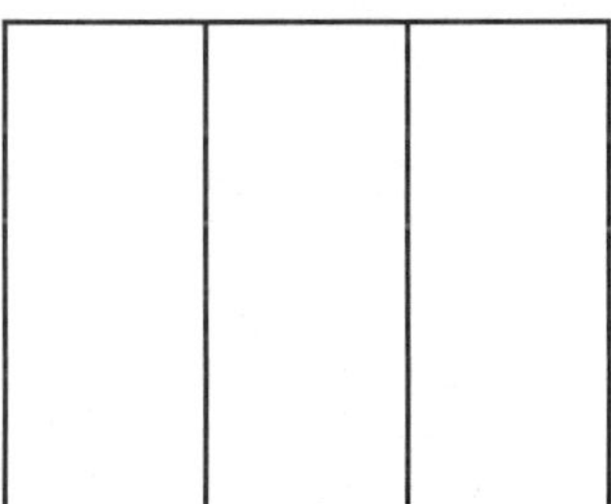

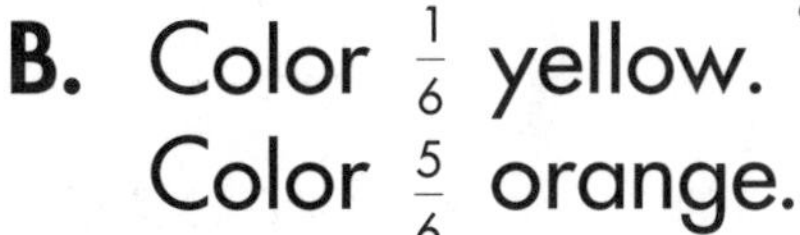

B. Color $\frac{1}{6}$ yellow.
Color $\frac{5}{6}$ orange.

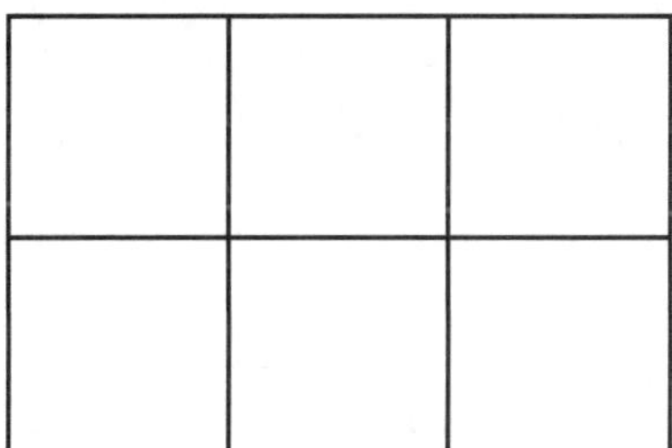

C. Color $\frac{1}{2}$ green.
Color $\frac{1}{2}$ yellow.

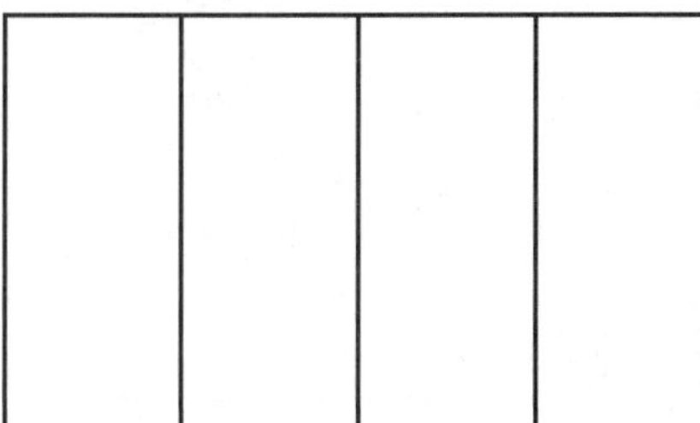

D. Color $\frac{1}{2}$ red.
Color $\frac{1}{2}$ yellow.

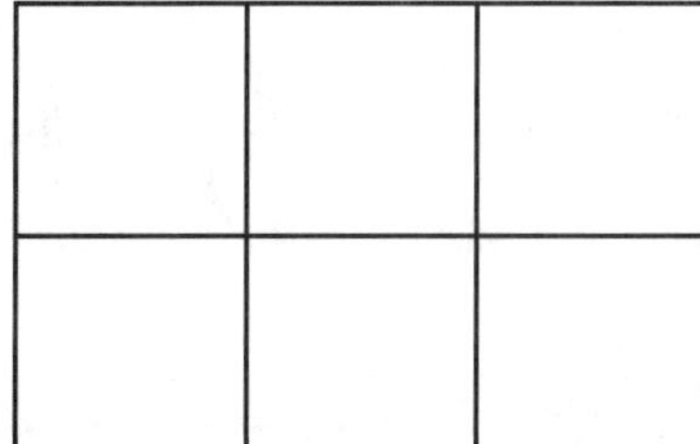

E. Color $\frac{1}{4}$ blue.
Color $\frac{1}{4}$ red.
Color $\frac{1}{2}$ yellow.

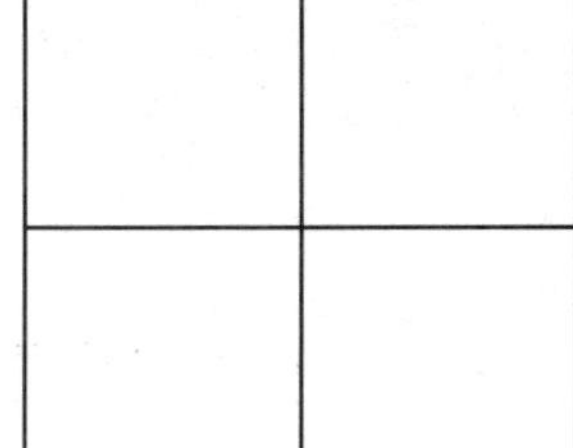

F. Color $\frac{1}{2}$ blue.
Color $\frac{1}{8}$ purple.
Color $\frac{3}{8}$ red.

Name ______________________ Date ____________

Fruity Halves

Visual Thinking

Color the pictures to match the fractions.

A. Color $\frac{1}{2}$ of the bananas.

$\frac{1}{2}$ of 4 = ________

B. Color $\frac{1}{2}$ of the oranges.

$\frac{1}{2}$ of 6 = ________

C. Color $\frac{1}{2}$ of the cherries

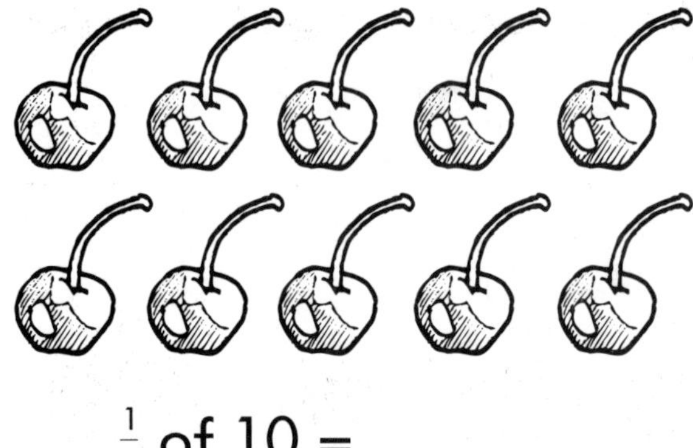

$\frac{1}{2}$ of 10 = ________

D. Color $\frac{1}{2}$ of the apples.

$\frac{1}{2}$ of 8 = ________

E. Color $\frac{1}{2}$ of the pineapples.

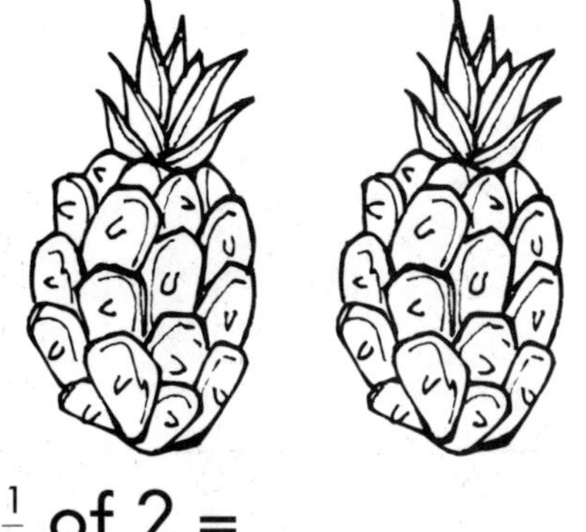

$\frac{1}{2}$ of 2 = ________

F. Color $\frac{1}{2}$ of the strawberries.

$\frac{1}{2}$ of 12 = ________

Name ______________________ Date ______________

Flower Sets

Visual Thinking

Circle the flowers to match the fractions.

A. Circle $\frac{1}{2}$.

B. Circle $\frac{1}{3}$.

C. Circle $\frac{1}{4}$.

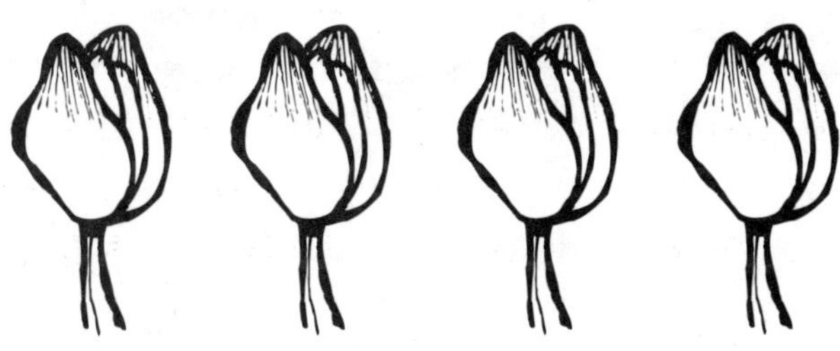

D. Circle $\frac{1}{2}$.

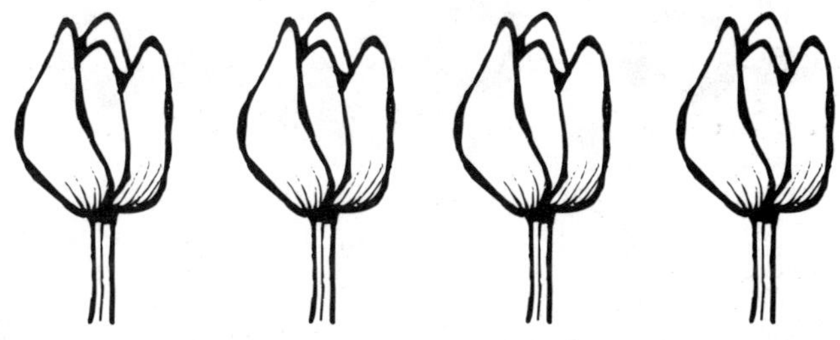

E. Circle $\frac{1}{3}$.

F. Circle $\frac{1}{4}$.

G. Circle $\frac{1}{3}$.

H. Circle $\frac{1}{2}$.

Name ______________________________ Date ______________

Toy Car Challenge

Use a Diagram

Jeff and Janet collect toy cars. Here are 6 of their cars. The cars come in three colors. Follow the directions to find out how many cars there are of each color.

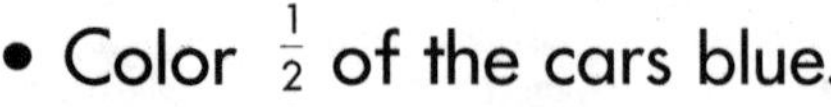

- Color $\frac{1}{2}$ of the cars blue.
- Color $\frac{1}{3}$ of the cars red.
- Color $\frac{1}{6}$ of the cars yellow.

How many cars are blue? __________

How many cars are red? __________

How many cars are yellow? __________

Try This! Suppose you colored $\frac{4}{6}$ of the cars purple instead. How many cars would be colored purple? __________

Name ______________________ Date ____________

Balloon Pairs

Use a Diagram

4 groups of **2** = **8**
4 × **2** = **8**

Multiply. Use the balloons at the right to help you.

A. 3 × 2 = _____ **F.** 4 × 2 = _____

B. 1 × 2 = _____ **G.** 7 × 2 = _____

C. 6 × 2 = _____ **H.** 5 × 2 = _____

D. 2 × 2 = _____ **I.** 10 × 2 = _____

E. 9 × 2 = _____ **J.** 8 × 2 = _____

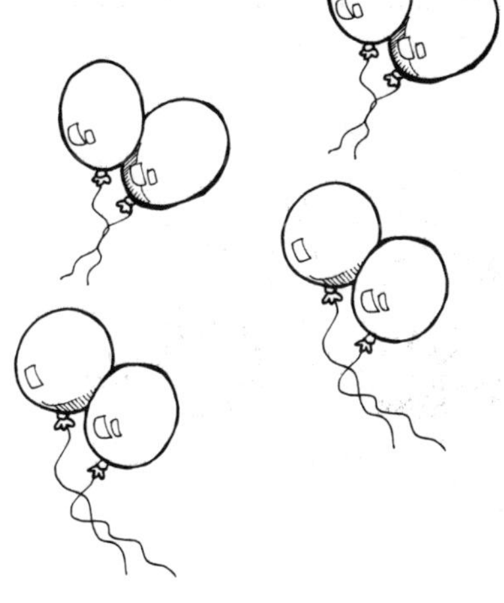

Look at your answers.
List them in order from the least to the greatest.

_____, _____, _____, _____, _____,

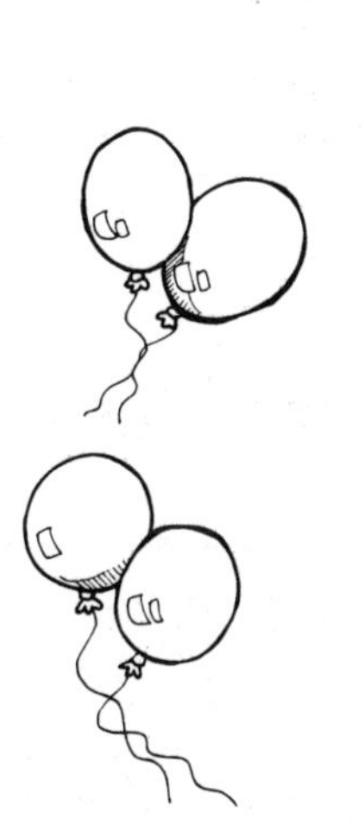

What pattern do you see?

____

____

Name ______________________ Date ____________

Draw and Multiply

Use a Diagram

Draw shapes to help you multiply.

A. 3 groups of 2

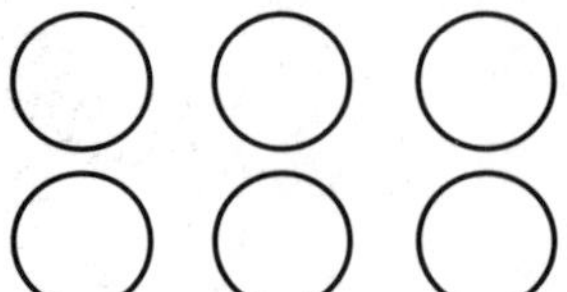

$3 \times 2 =$ ________

B. 2 groups of 5

$2 \times 5 =$ ________

C. 5 groups of 2

$5 \times 2 =$ ________

D. 3 groups of 4

$3 \times 4 =$ ________

E. 5 groups of 3

$5 \times 3 =$ ________

F. 2 groups of 10

$2 \times 10 =$ ________

G. 3 groups of 3

$3 \times 3 =$ ________

H. 4 groups of 4

$4 \times 4 =$ ________

Name ______________________________ Date ______________

Critter Math

Find a Pattern

Write a multiplication fact to solve each problem. Use the pictures to help you.

A. With 1 ladybug, how many legs are there?

____

B. With 3 ladybugs, how many legs are there?

____

C. With 5 ladybugs, how many legs are there?

____

D. With 1 bee, how many stripes are there?

____

E. With 2 bees, how many stripes are there?

____

F. With 6 bees, how many stripes are there?

____

G. With 1 spider, how many legs are there?

____

H. With 2 spiders, how many legs are there?

____

I. With 3 spiders, how many legs are there?

____

Name ______________________________ Date ______________

High-Flying Kites

Guess and Check

Use the numbers on the kites to write multiplication facts. Write the facts on the clouds.

A.

4 × 3 = 12

B.

_____ × _____ = _____

C.

_____ × _____ = _____

D.

_____ × _____ = _____

E.

_____ × _____ = _____

F.

_____ × _____ = _____

G.

_____ × _____ = _____

H.

_____ × _____ = _____

Name ______________________ Date ____________

Missing Shapes

Find and Extend a Pattern

Draw the missing shapes to complete each pattern.

A.

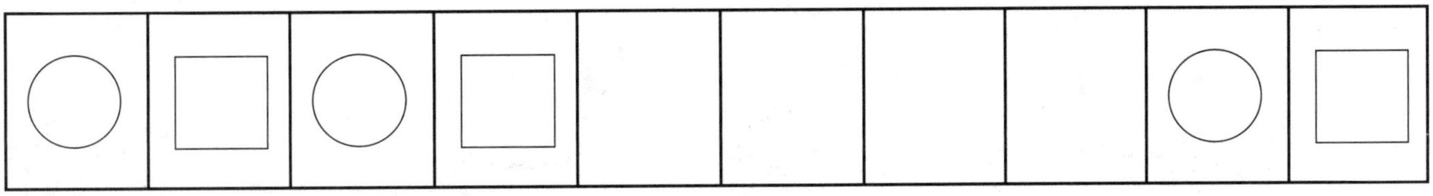

B.

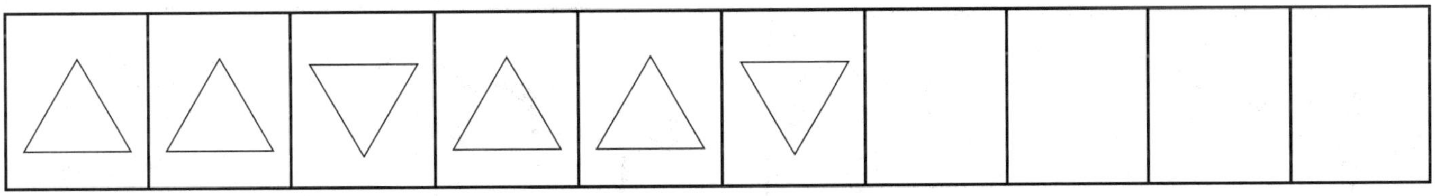

C.

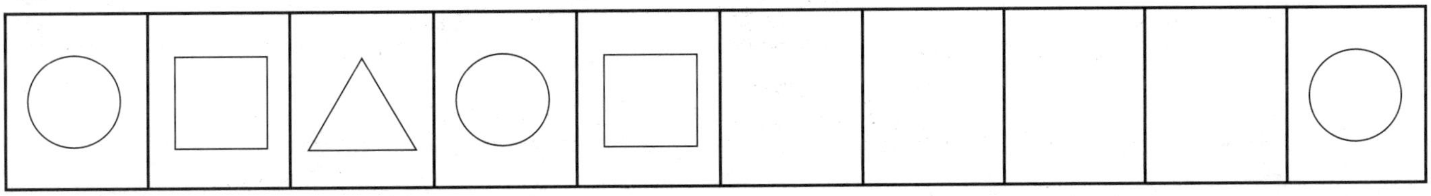

D.

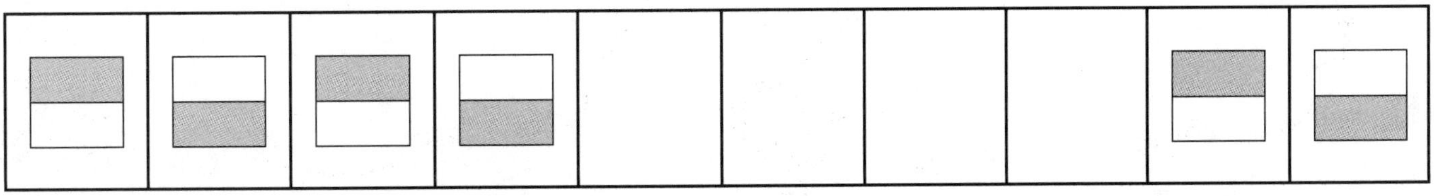

E.

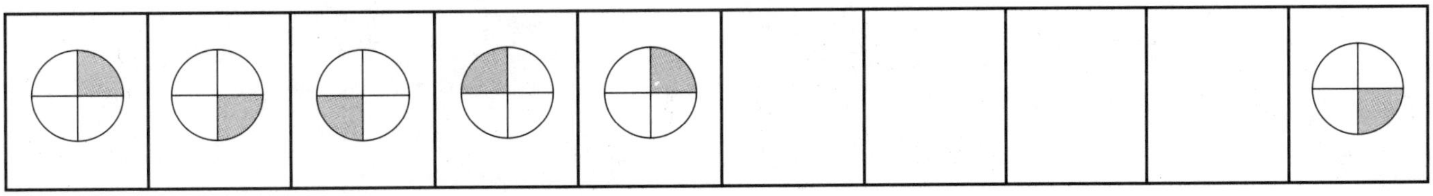

Name ______________________________ Date ______________

Pretty Beads

Find and Extend a Pattern

Draw designs on the beads to complete each pattern.

A.

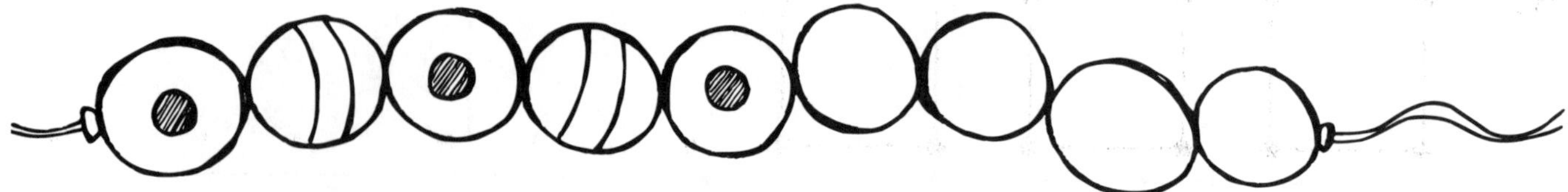

B.

C.

D.

E.

Name ______________________ Date ____________

Dot-to-Dots

Find and Extend a Pattern

Connect the dots to extend each pattern.

A.

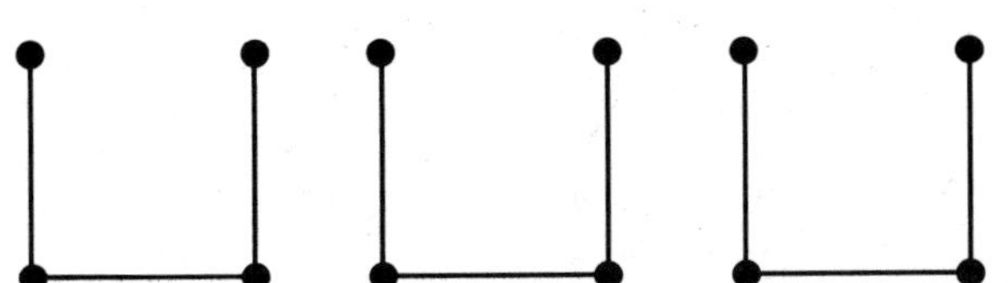

B.

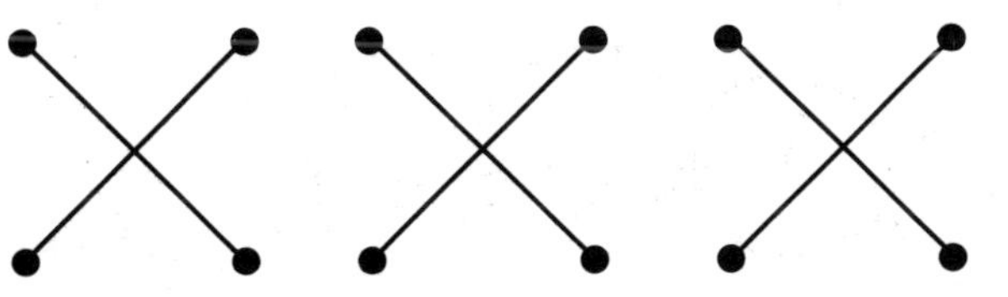

C.

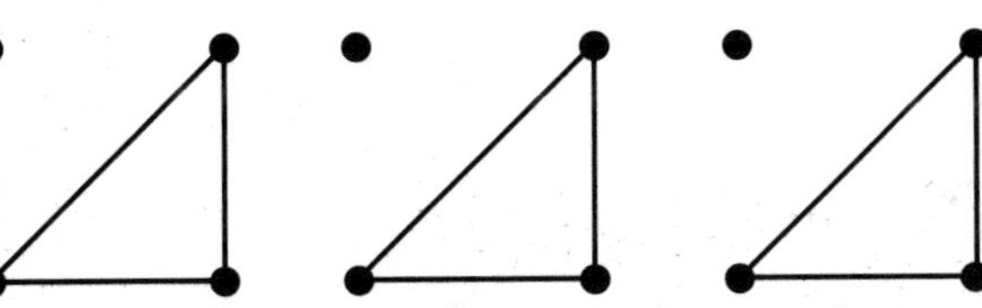

D.

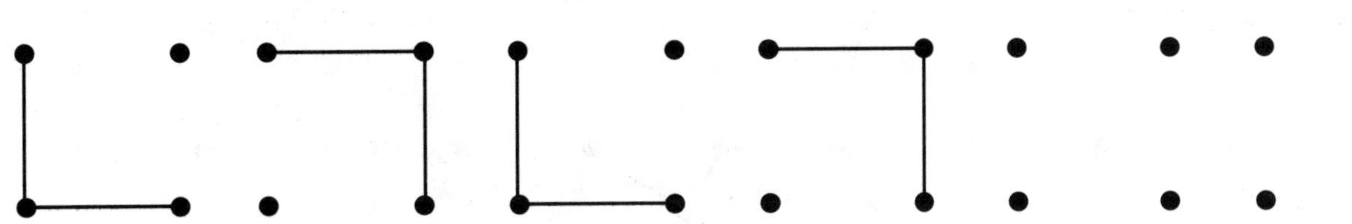

Connect the dots to make your own pattern.

E.

Name ______________________________ Date ______________

Dots and Lines

Find and Extend a Pattern

Connect the dots to extend each pattern.

A.

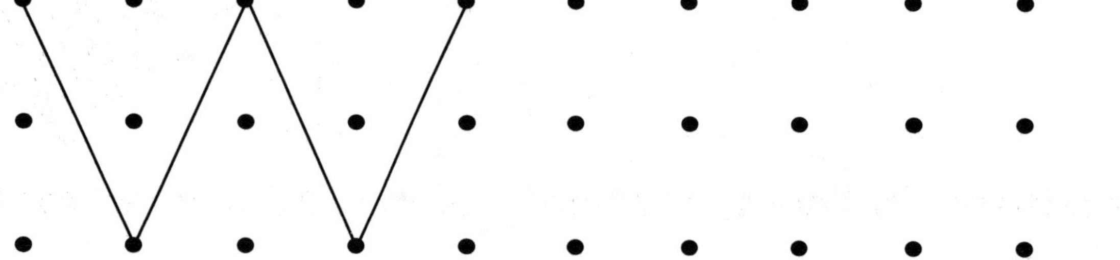

B.

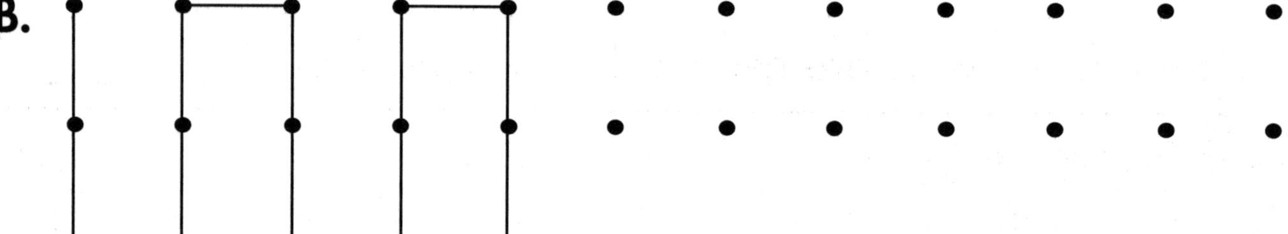

C.

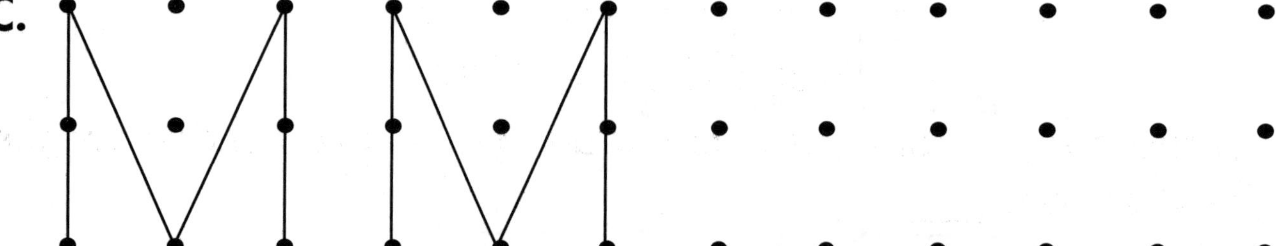

D.

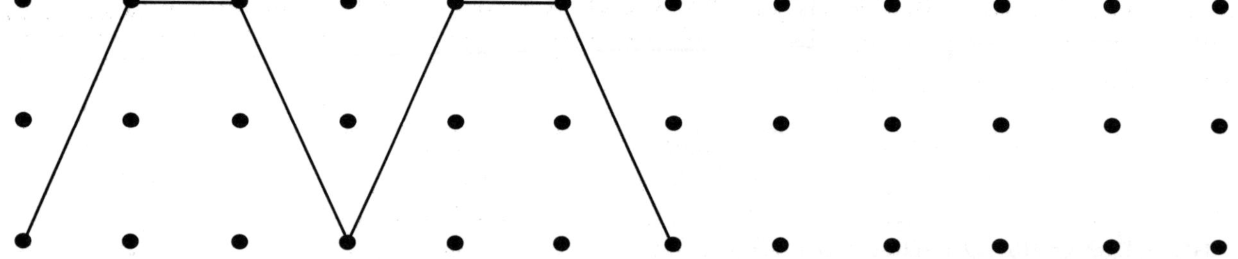

E.

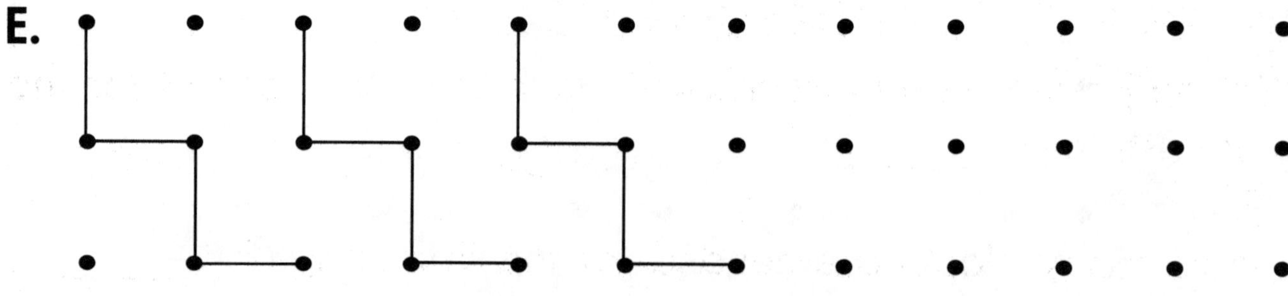

Name ______________________________ Date ______________

Block Patterns

Find and Extend a Pattern

Look at the pattern of blocks.

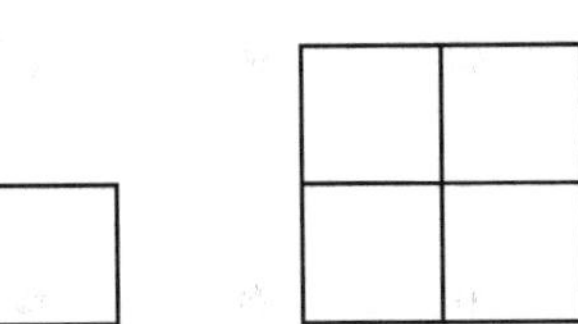

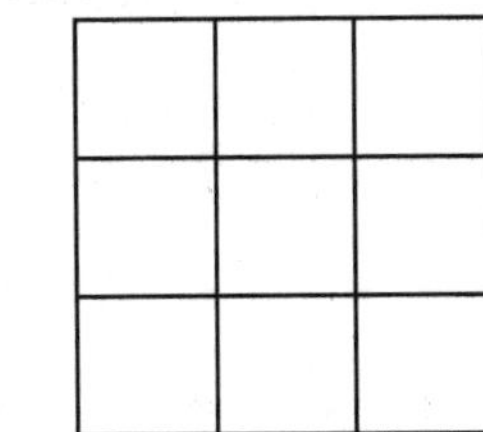

A. If the pattern continues, how many blocks are needed for the next shape? _______

B. How many blocks are needed for the fifth shape? _______

Look at the pattern of blocks.

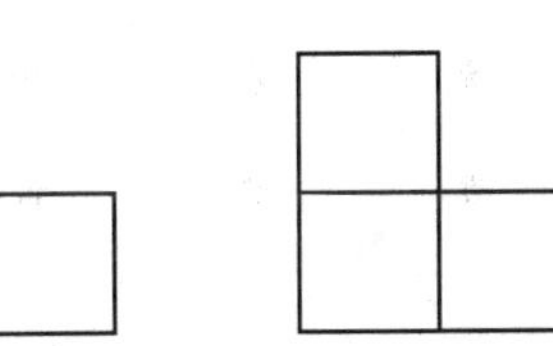

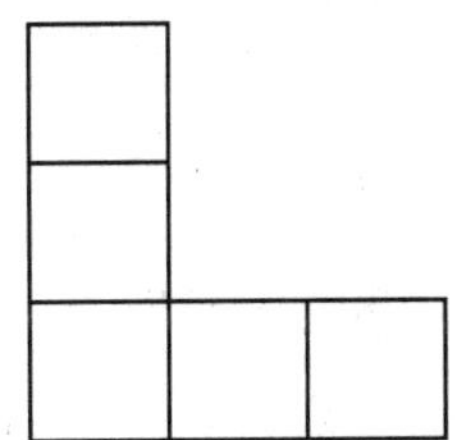

C. If the pattern continues, how many blocks are needed for the next shape? _______

D. How many blocks are needed for the fifth shape? _______

Look at the pattern of blocks.

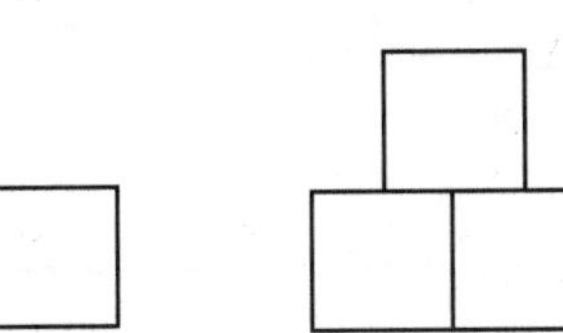

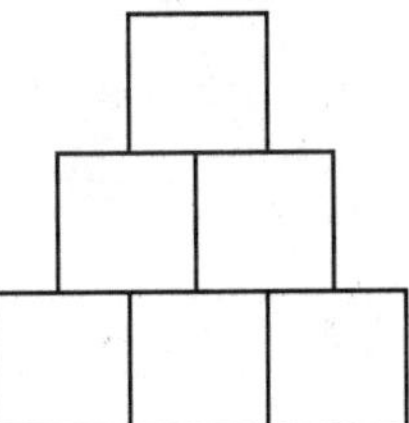

E. If the pattern continues, how many blocks are needed for the next shape? _______

F. How many blocks are needed for the fifth shape? _______

Name ______________________ Date __________

Caterpillar Counting

Find and Extend a Pattern

Look at each pattern. Write the missing numbers.

A.

What is the pattern? ______________________

B.

What is the pattern? ______________________

C.

What is the pattern? ______________________

D.

What is the pattern? ______________________

E.

What is the pattern? ______________________

Name ______________________ Date ____________

Number Patterns

Find and Extend a Pattern

Look at the number patterns.
Write the missing numbers in each row.

A. 10, 20, 30, 40, 50, ______, ______, ______, ______

B. 11, 22, 33, 44, 55, ______, ______, ______, ______

C. 5, 15, 25, 35, 45, 55, ______, ______, ______, ______

D. 12, 23, 34, 45, ______, ______, ______, ______

E. 1, 2, 1, 3, 1, 4, 1, 5, ______, ______, ______, ______

F. 1, 10, 2, 20, 3, 30, 4, ______, ______, ______, ______

G. 1, 2, 2, 3, 3, 3, 4, 4, 4, 4, ______, ______, ______, ______

Make up your own number pattern.

____

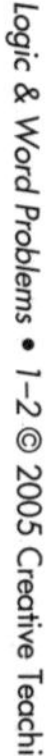

Name ______________________ Date ____________

Dru's Clues

Find and Extend a Pattern

Dru wrote some number riddles. Read the clues. Write the answer to each riddle.

A. The number is greater than 40 and less than 60. Count by tens, and you say the number. The number is _____.

B. The number is greater than 60 and less than 70. Count by fives, and you say the number. The number is _____.

C. The number is greater than 35 and less than 45. Count by fives, and you say the number. The number is _____.

D. The number is greater than 12 and less than 16. Count by twos, and you say the number. The number is _____.

E. The number is greater than 15 and less than 20. Count by threes, and you say the number. The number is _____.

F. The number is greater than 20 and less than 25. Count by fours, and you say the number. The number is _____.

Name ______________________ Date ____________

Frog Jumps

Organize Information

Freddy Frog jumps on every third lily pad. Write **F** on the lily pads he lands on. Hoppy Frog jumps on every fourth lily pad. Write **H** on the lily pads he lands on.

A. How many lily pads does Freddy land on? ____________

B. How many lily pads does Hoppy land on? ____________

C. Write the numbers of the lily pads that Freddy and Hoppy both land on.

____

Name ______________________ Date ______________

Make Them Equal

Draw a Diagram

Fill in the missing numbers. Draw pictures to help you.

A. 3 + 3 = 2 + ___4___

| | | | |

| | | | | | |

B. 4 + 3 = 5 + ______

C. ______ + 6 = 3 + 5

D. ______ + 4 = 7 + 3

E. 8 + 4 = ______ + 3

F. 3 + 6 = ______ + 7

G. 4 + ______ = 3 + 8

H. 7 + ______ = 6 + 6

I. 5 + 4 = 6 + ______

J. 3 + ______ = 4 + 8

Name ______________________________ Date ______________

A Balancing Act

Guess and Check

Fill in the missing numbers that will help keep the facts balanced.

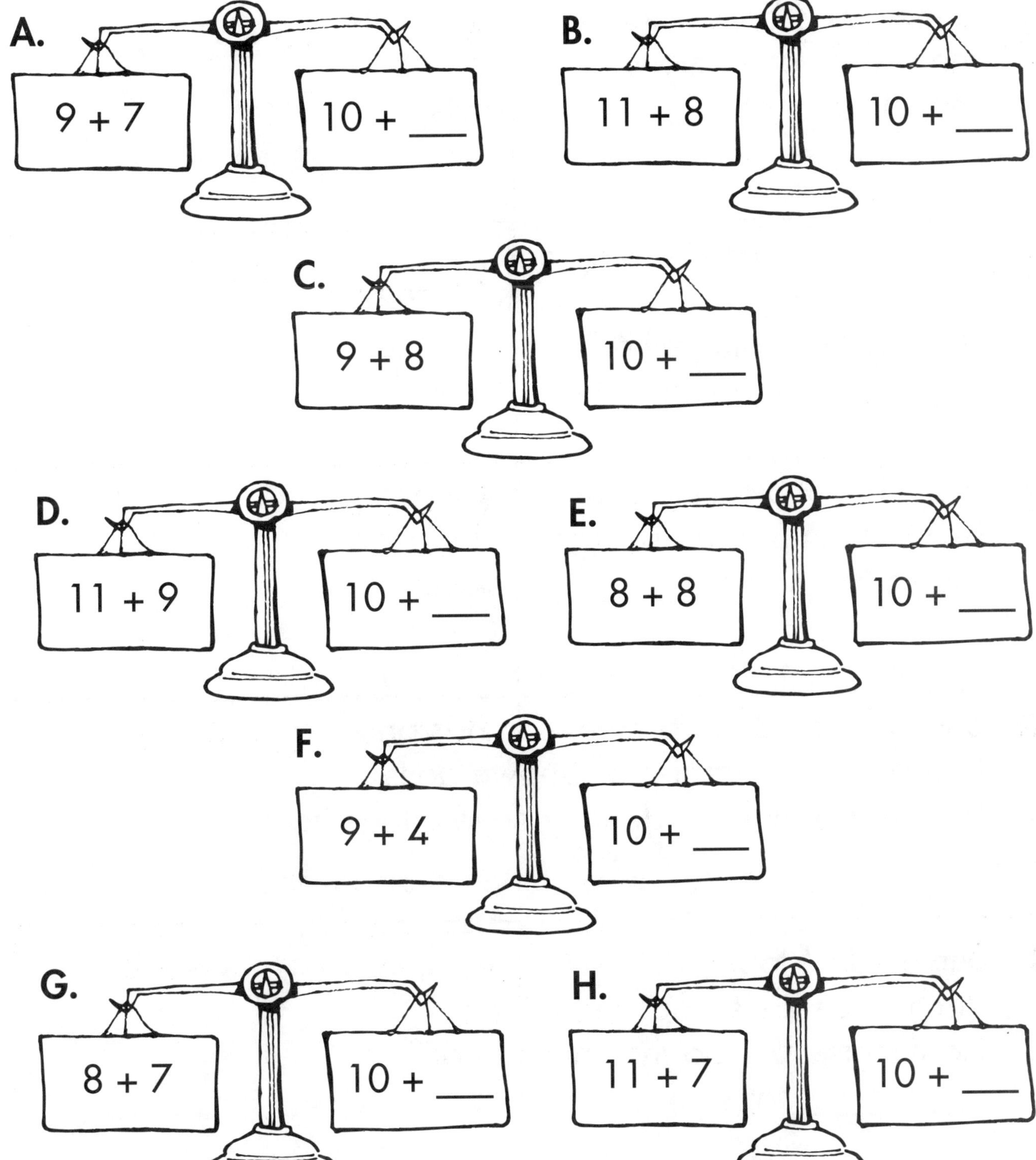

Name ______________________ Date __________

Playtime

Draw a Diagram

Solve the problems. Draw pictures to help you.

A. Linda has 7 balls. Joe has 2 more balls than Linda does. How many balls do they have in all? ___16___ balls

B. Kristi has 8 markers. Meg has 2 less markers than Kristi. How many markers do they have altogether?
__________ markers

C. Brian has 9 blocks. Nicky has 4 more blocks than Brian. How many blocks do they have in all? __________ blocks

D. Shawn has 12 marbles. Simon has only half as many marbles as Shawn does. How many marbles do they have altogether?
__________ marbles

E. Jesse has 7 tops.
Rachel has 2 less tops than Jesse.
How many tops do they have in all?
__________ tops

Name ______________________ Date ____________

Snack Time

Draw a Diagram

Solve the problems. Draw pictures to help you.

A. There are 9 apples. They are red and green. For every red apple, there are 2 green apples.

How many apples are red? ______
How many apples are green? ______

B. There are pears, oranges, and bananas in a bowl. There are 12 fruits in all. There are twice as many pears as there are oranges. There is the same number of bananas and oranges.

How many pears are there? ______
How many oranges are there? ______
How many bananas are there? ______

C. There are 12 cookies with orange, yellow, and green frosting. There are 2 more green cookies than yellow cookies. There are 2 more orange cookies than green cookies.

How many cookies are yellow? ______
How many cookies are green? ______
How many cookies are orange? ______

Name ______________________________ Date ____________

At the Park

Use Objects, Draw a Diagram, Guess and Check

Read the clues. Solve the problems.

A. There are more than 16 birds in a tree.
There are less than 20 birds in the tree.
The birds can be put into groups of 3.
How many birds are there? ______

B. There are more than 20 children at the park.
There are less than 30 children at the park.
The children can be put into groups of 6.
How many children are there? ______

C. There are 20 parents at the park.
There are 4 more mothers than fathers.
How many mothers and fathers are there?
______ mothers ______ fathers

D. There are 8 children on the swings.
That is 2 less than the number of children in the sand.
How many children are on the swings and in the sand?
______

E. There are 16 red, yellow, and purple flowers by a bench.
There are 4 more yellow flowers than red flowers.
There are 2 more purple flowers than yellow flowers.
How many are there of each flower?
red ______ yellow ______ purple ______

Name ______________________________ Date ______________

A Three-Horned Fellow

Find and Extend a Pattern, Interpret Information

Triceratops was a dinosaur. It had 3 horns on its head.
Fill in the chart. Then answer the questions.

Number of Triceratops	Number of Horns in All

A. How many horns did 2 triceratops have in all? ________

B. How many horns did 5 triceratops have in all? ________

C. How many more horns would 4 triceratops have than 3 triceratops? ______

D. If there were 6 triceratops, how many horns would there be in all? _______

E. What pattern do you see on the chart? ____________________

____

Name ______________________________ Date ______________

Looking for Shells

Collect and Organize Information

Four children were at the beach looking for shells. They put their shells in a bucket.

A. Each time Brad put 1 shell in the bucket, Joni put in 2. They had 15 shells in all. How many shells did each child have? Fill in the chart to help you solve the problem.

	Number of Shells Found Each Time					Total Number
Brad	1					
Joni	2					

Brad found _____ shells. Joni found _____ shells.

B. Each time Lynn put in 2 shells, Mike put in 3. They found 25 shells in all. How many shells did each child find? Fill in the chart to help you solve the problem.

	Number of Shells Found Each Time					Total Number
Lynn						
Mike						

Lynn found _____ shells. Mike found _____ shells.

Name ______________________ Date ____________

Math Field Trip

Collect and Organize Information

Fill in the charts to solve the problems.

A. On Monday, 5 classes went to the zoo. Every day after that, the number of classes was 2 more than the day before. How many classes visited the zoo on Friday?

	Monday	Tuesday	Wednesday	Thursday	Friday
Number of Classes	5				

______ classes visited the zoo on Friday.

B. On Monday, 2 classes went to a museum. Every day after that, the number of classes doubled. How many classes visited the museum on Friday?

	Monday	Tuesday	Wednesday	Thursday	Friday
Number of Classes					

______ classes visited the museum on Friday.

C. The number of classes at the beach went up by 5 each day. If 30 classes went to the beach on Friday, how many classes went on Monday?

	Monday	Tuesday	Wednesday	Thursday	Friday
Number of Classes					

______ classes went to the beach on Monday.

Name ________________________________ Date ____________

Here Comes the Circus!

Logical Thinking, Guess and Check

Who's in the circus parade? Solve the problems to find out!

A. Steve counted the jugglers and bears in the parade. He counted 4 heads and 12 legs. How many jugglers and bears were there?

______ jugglers ______ bears

B. Lori counted the clowns and elephants in the parade. She counted 7 heads and 20 legs. How many clowns and elephants were there?

______ clowns ______ elephants

C. Matt counted the lion tamers and lions in the parade. He counted 5 heads and 16 legs. How many lion tamers and lions were there?

______ lion tamers ______ lions

D. Chelsea counted the acrobats and horses in the parade. She counted 8 heads and 24 legs. How many acrobats and horses were there?

______ acrobats ______ horses

Name ______________________________ Date ______________

Zoo Clues

Logical Thinking, Guess and Check

Read the clues to find out how many zoo animals the children saw.

A. Cindy saw some parrots and camels.
She counted 4 heads and 12 feet.
How many parrots and camels did
Cindy see?

______ parrots

______ camels

B. Evan saw some ostriches and hippos.
He counted 5 heads and 14 feet.
How many ostriches and hippos did
Evan see?

______ ostriches

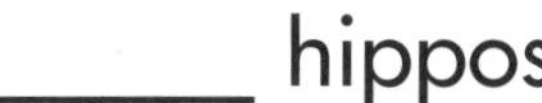
______ hippos

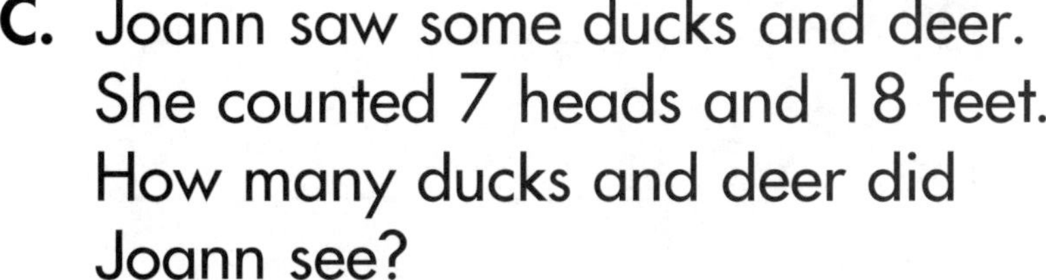
C. Joann saw some ducks and deer.
She counted 7 heads and 18 feet.
How many ducks and deer did
Joann see?

______ ducks

______ deer

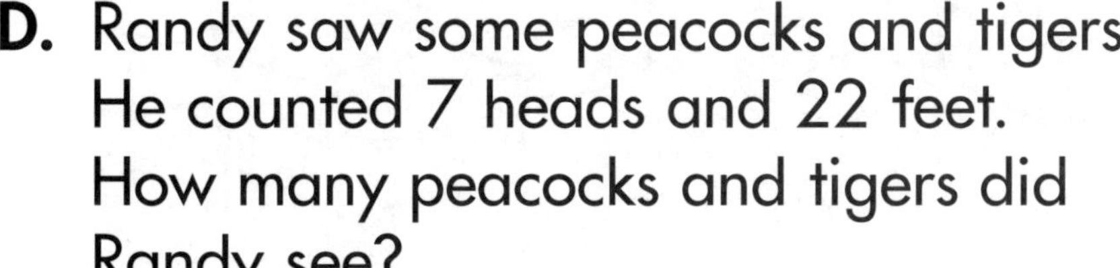
D. Randy saw some peacocks and tigers.
He counted 7 heads and 22 feet.
How many peacocks and tigers did
Randy see?

______ peacocks

______ tigers

Name ______________________ Date ______________

Ricky's Rocks

Logical Thinking

Ricky collects rocks. He keeps them in round boxes and square boxes. All of the round boxes have the same number of rocks. All of the square boxes have the same number of rocks.

Look at the clues. Find out how many rocks are in each box.

= 14 rocks

= 12 rocks

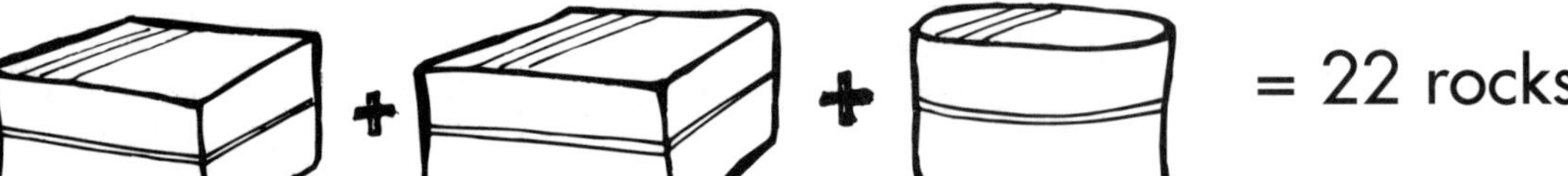

= 22 rocks

How many rocks are in the round box? ______________

How many rocks are in the square box? ______________

Look at the sets of boxes below.

Set 1

Set 2

Which set has more rocks—Set 1 or Set 2? Explain your answer.

____

Name ______________________ Date ____________

Who's Who?

Logical Thinking

Read the clues. Write each child's name under the correct picture.

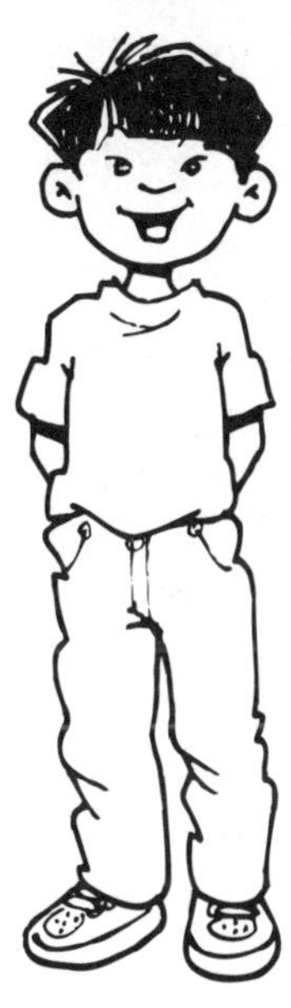

A.

Clues

- Sid is taller than Jim.
- Tom is taller than Jim.
- Sid is taller than Tom.

__________ __________ __________

B.

Clues

- Sue is taller than Dee.
- Bev is taller than Jan.
- Jan is taller than Sue.

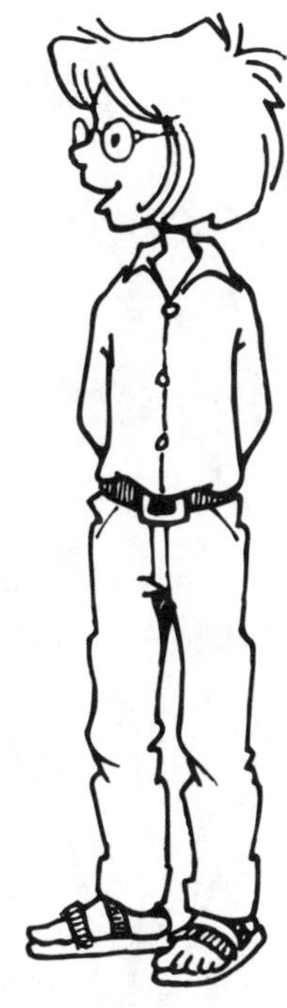

__________ __________ __________ __________

Name ______________________ Date ____________

A Flower Garden

Logical Thinking

There are 6 flowers in the garden.
They are red, yellow, or orange.

Read the clues.
Then color the flowers.

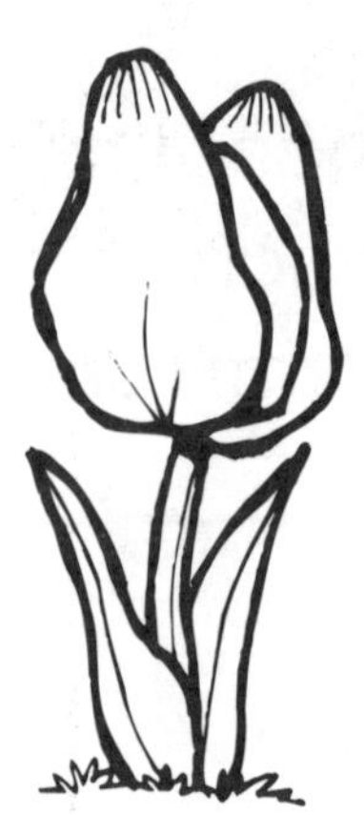

Clues

There are more red flowers than orange flowers.

There are more yellow flowers than red flowers.

Name ______________________ Date ____________

Colorful Flowers

Logical Thinking

Billy and Janey have 9 flowers in their garden.
The flowers are red, purple, blue, and yellow.

Read the clues.
Then color the flowers.

Clues

There are more red flowers than purple flowers.

There are more blue flowers than red flowers.

There is the same number of blue and yellow flowers.

Name ______________________ Date ____________

Bear Buddies

Logical Thinking

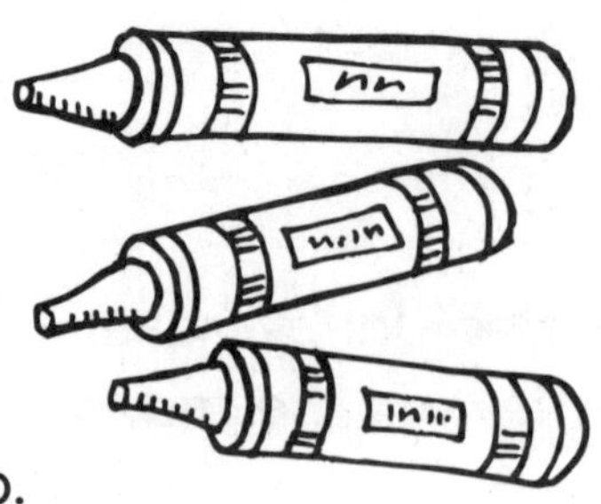

There are 6 teddy bears. Each one is a different color.
Read the clues. Find out which bears are together.
Then color the pictures to show how the bears are paired up.

Clues

The brown bear is with either the yellow bear or the black bear.

The orange bear is with either the black bear or the purple bear.

The blue bear is with the purple bear.

Name ______________________________ Date ______________

All in the Family

Logical Thinking

Solve the problems.

A. Jim is 3 years older than his sister Kim.
Their ages add up to 13.

How old is Jim? _______

How old is Kim? _______

B. Sandy and Mandy are twins.
In two years, their ages will add up to 18.

How old are the twins today? _______

C. Meg's mom is twice as old as Meg.
Together, their ages add up to 60.

How old is Meg? ______

How old is Meg's mom? ______

D. Cory's dad is three times as old as Cory.
Cory's grandfather is two times the age of Corey's dad.
The ages of Cory, his dad, and his grandfather add up to 100.

How old is Cory? _______
How old is Cory's dad? _______
How old is Cory's grandfather? ______

Name ______________________________ Date ______________

Sides and Corners

Use a Diagram

Look at each shape.
Count the number of sides and corners.

A.

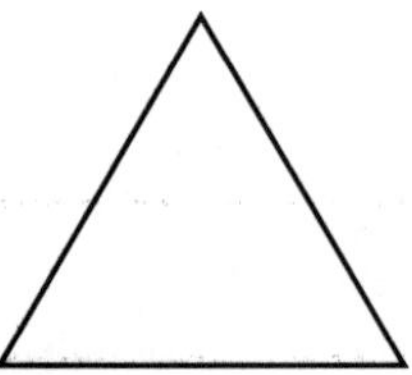

______ sides

______ corners

B.

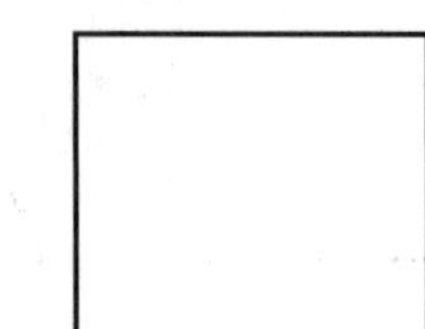

______ sides

______ corners

C.

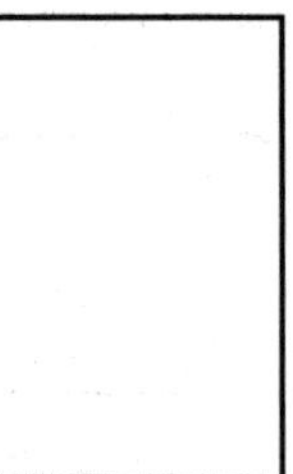

______ sides

______ corners

D.

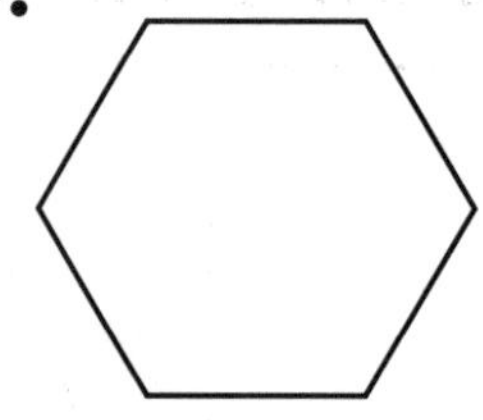

______ sides

______ corners

E.

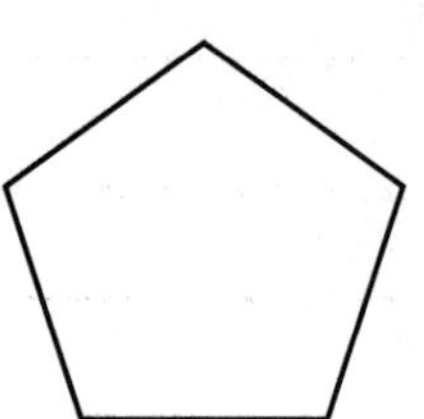

______ sides

______ corners

F.

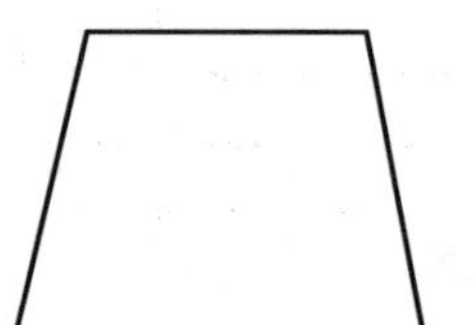

______ sides

______ corners

What can you say about the number of sides and corners a shape has?

____

Name ______________________________ Date ______________

Faces and Shapes

Visual Thinking

Look at each solid. Look at its shaded face. Color the shape that matches the face.

A.

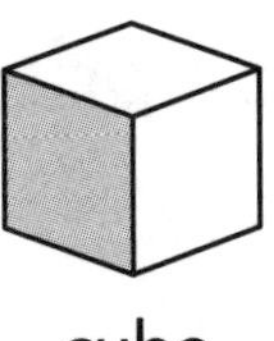

cube

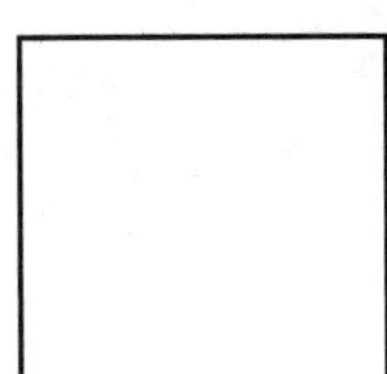 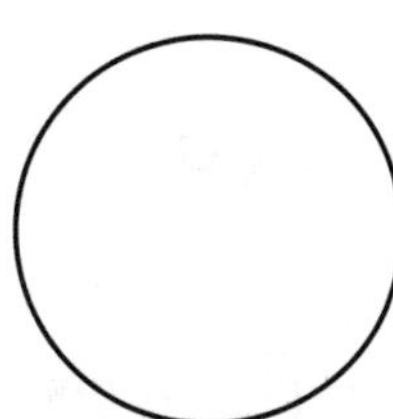

B.

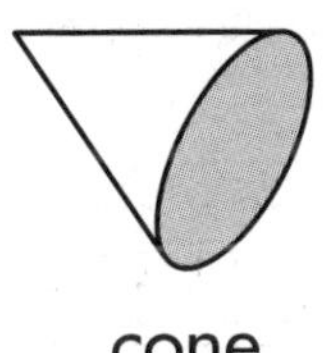

cone

  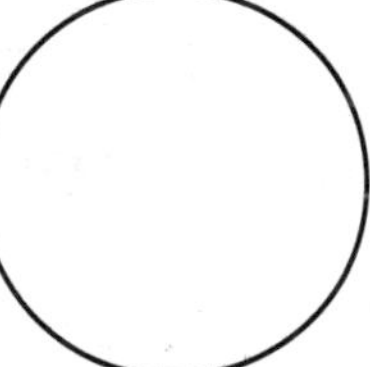 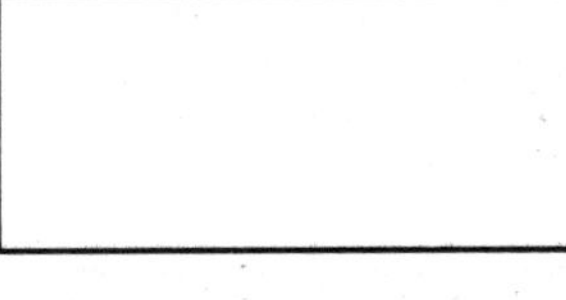

C.

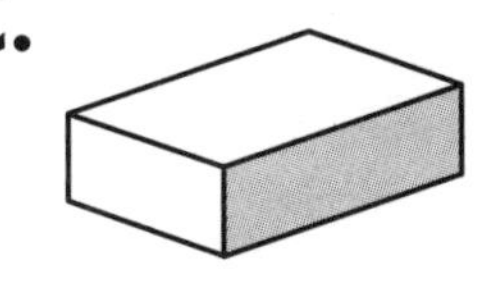

rectangular prism

 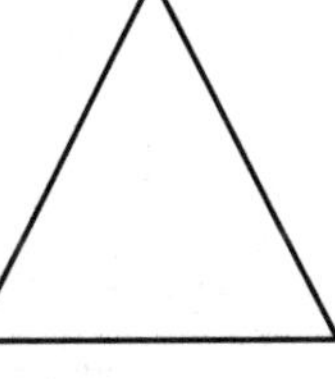 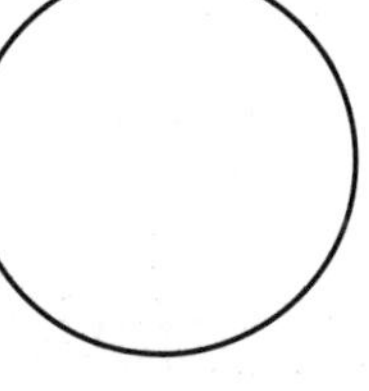 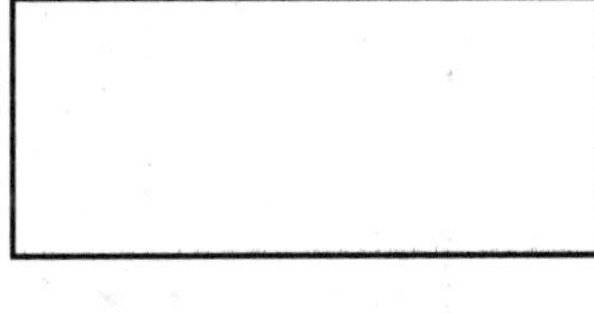

D.

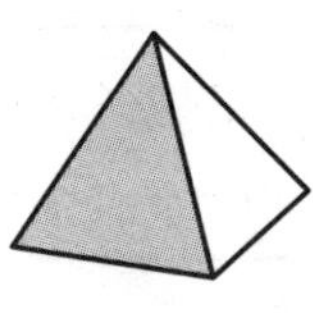

pyramid

  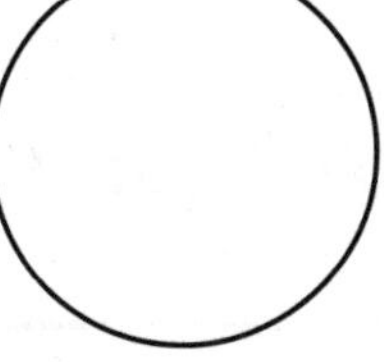 

E.

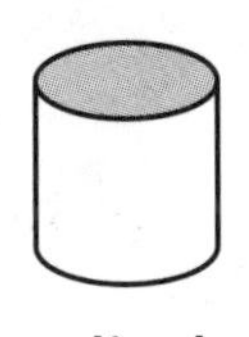

cylinder

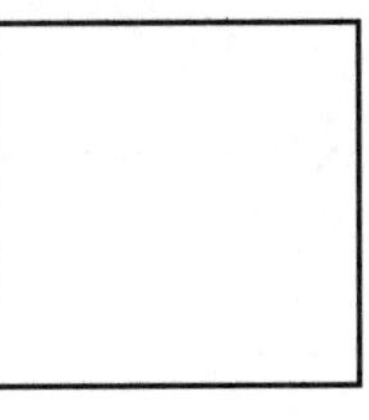 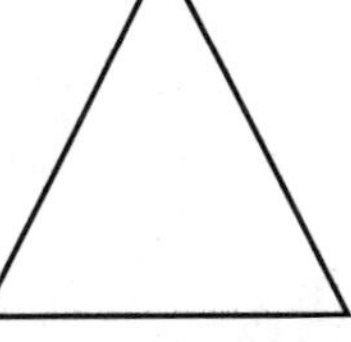 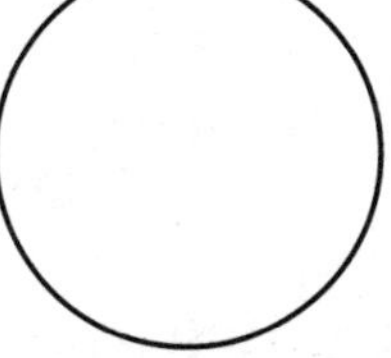 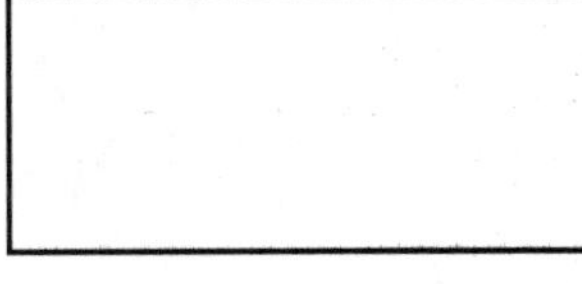

F.

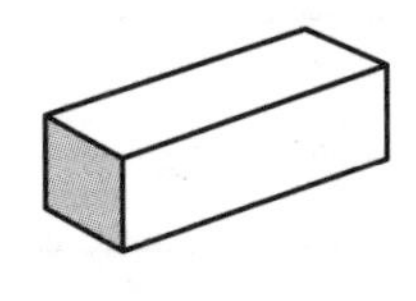

rectangular prism

 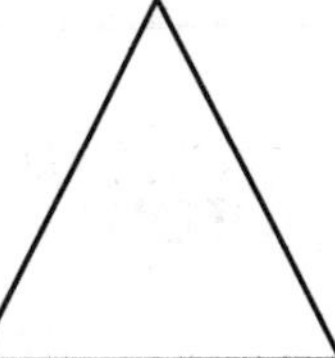 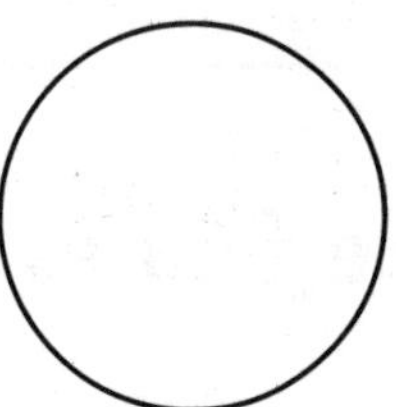 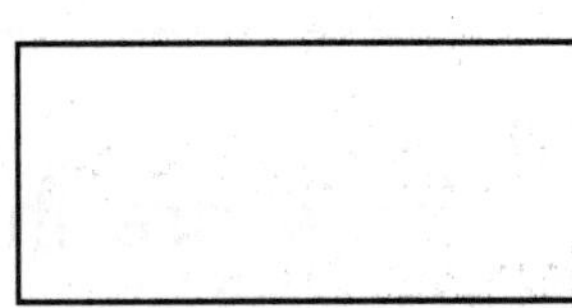

Name ______________________ Date ____________

Alike and Different

Visual Thinking

Compare the two figures in each row. Write how they are alike and different.

A.

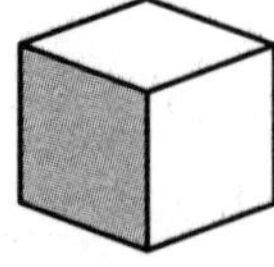

cube

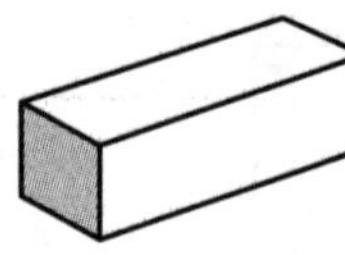

rectangular prism

How are these figures alike? ______________________

____

How are these figures different? ______________________

____

B.

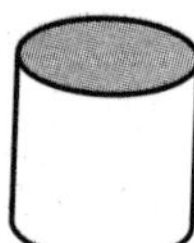

cylinder

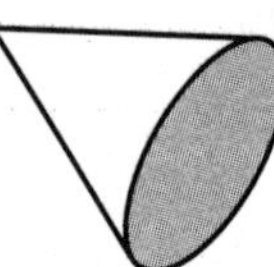

cone

How are these figures alike? ______________________

____

How are these figures different? ______________________

____

C.

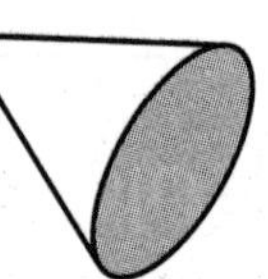

cone

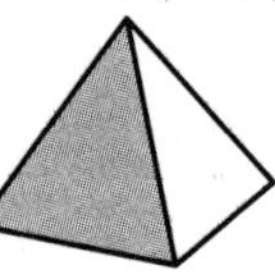

pyramid

How are these figures alike? ______________________

____

How are these figures different? ______________________

____

Name ______________________________ Date ______________

Sorting Shapes

Visual Thinking

Tell how the shapes in each group are alike. Draw another shape that belongs in the group. Then draw a shape that does not belong.

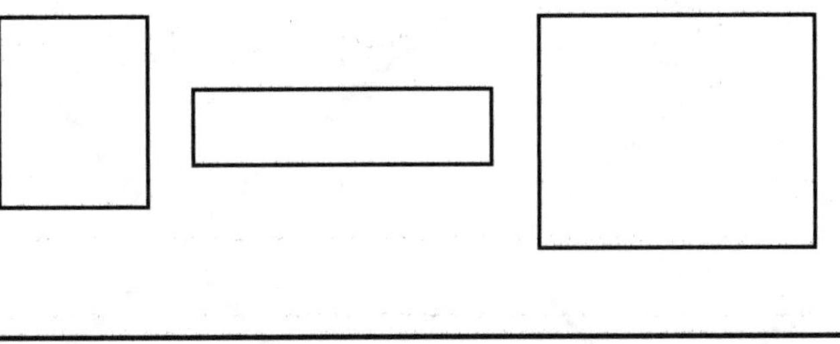

____

____

Belongs	Does Not Belong

B.

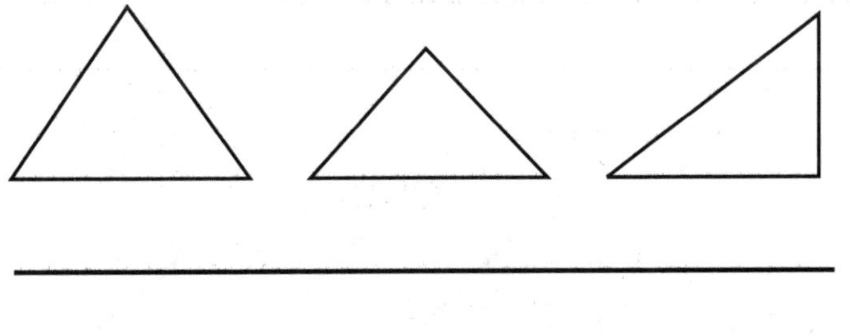

____

____

Belongs	Does Not Belong

C.

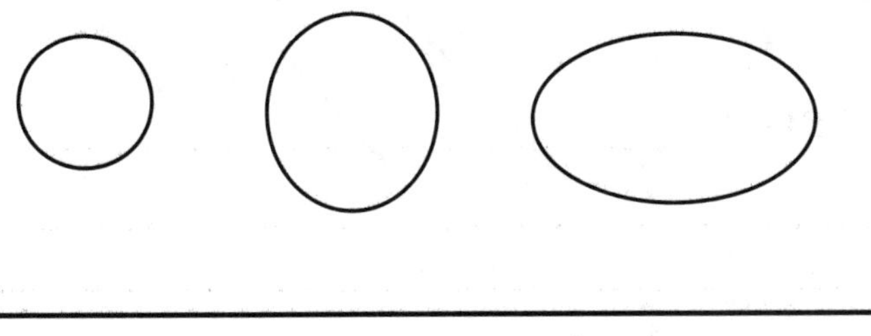

____

____

Belongs	Does Not Belong

D.

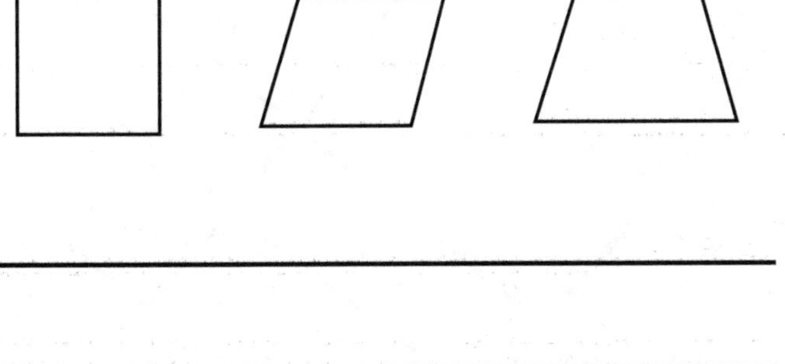

____

____

Belongs	Does Not Belong

Name ______________________________ Date ______________

Fishy Squares

Visual Thinking

Count the squares in each fish. Be careful! Some squares are hidden.

A. How many squares do you see in this fish?

________ squares

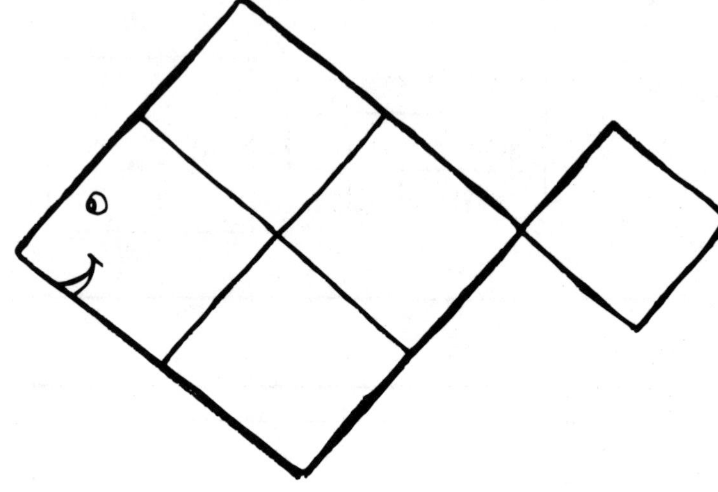

B. How many squares do you see in this fish?

________ squares

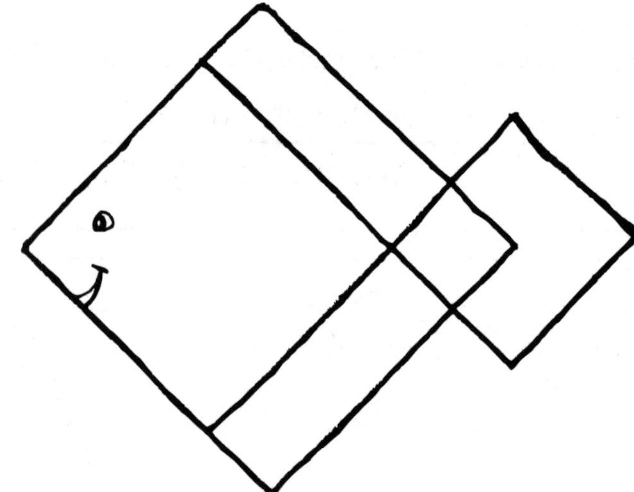

C. How many squares do you see in this fish?

________ squares

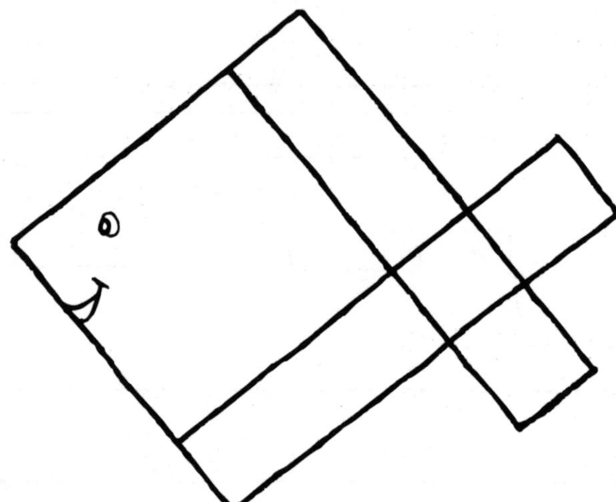

Name ______________________ Date ____________

Tricky Triangles

Visual Thinking

Count the triangles. Don't get fooled!

A. How many triangles do you see in this design?
________ triangles

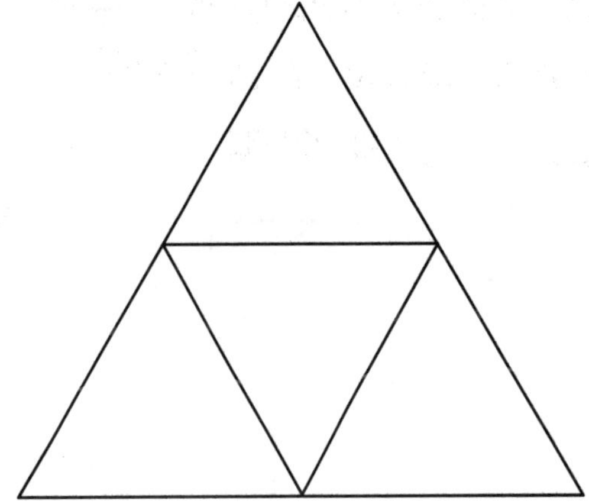

B. How many triangles do you see in this design?
________ triangles

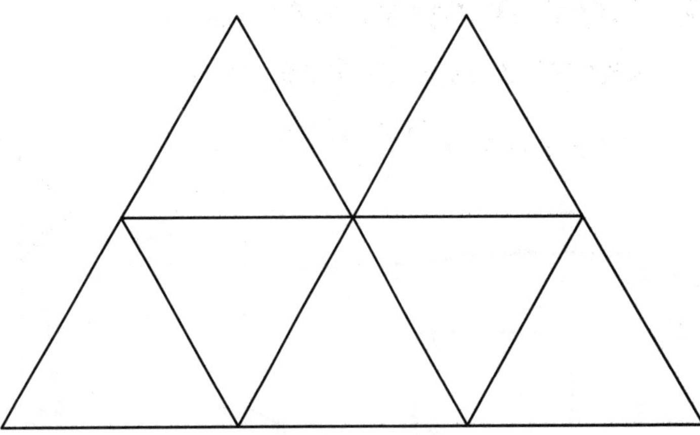

C. How many triangles do you see in this design?
________ triangles

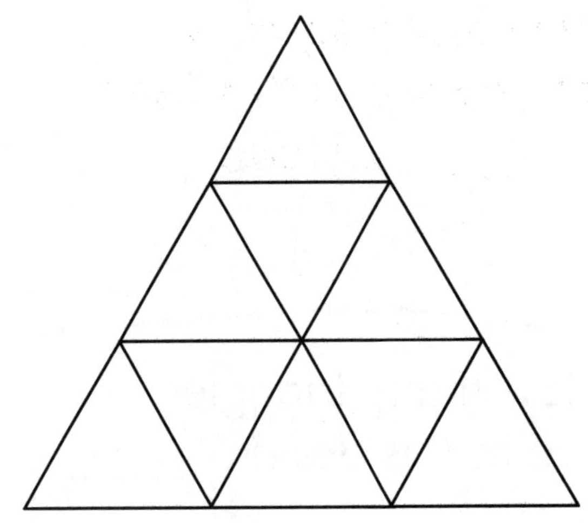

Name ______________________________ Date ______________

Shape Designs

Visual Thinking

Mrs. Turner's class made shape designs. Some of their designs are shown below.

A.

How many squares are in this design? _____

B.

How many circles are in this design? _____

C.

How many triangles are in this design? _____

D.

How many rectangles are in this design? ______

Name ______________________ Date ____________

Find the Shape

Visual Thinking

Color the squares in the rectangles to show each shape.

A.

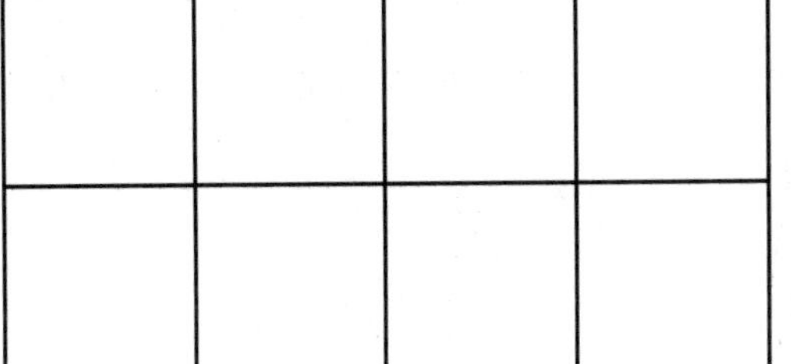

B.

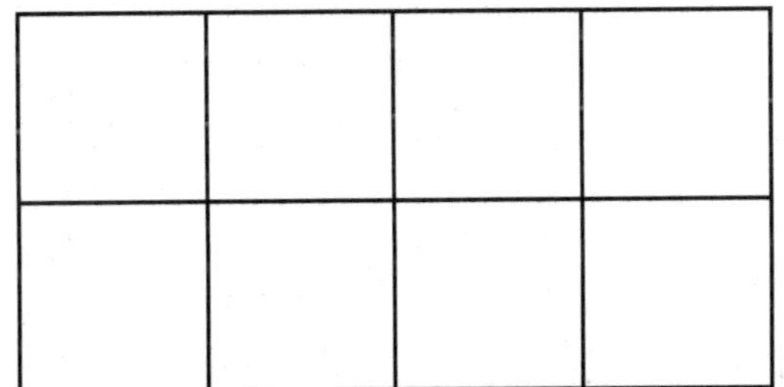

C.

D.

E.

Name ______________________ Date ____________

Hide and Seek

Visual Thinking

Look at each set of pictures. Study the shape on the left. Find it on the right. Then color it.

A.

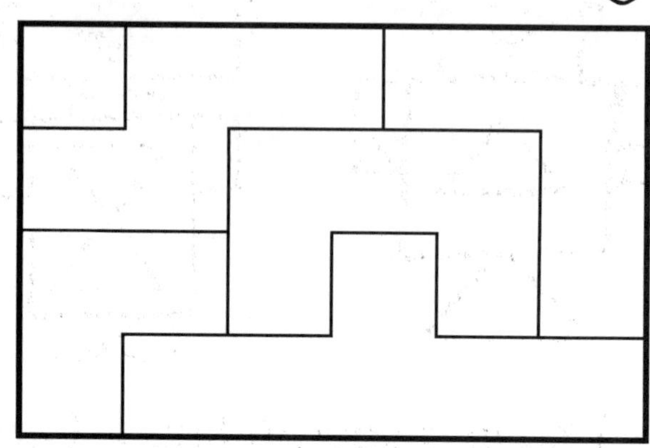

B.

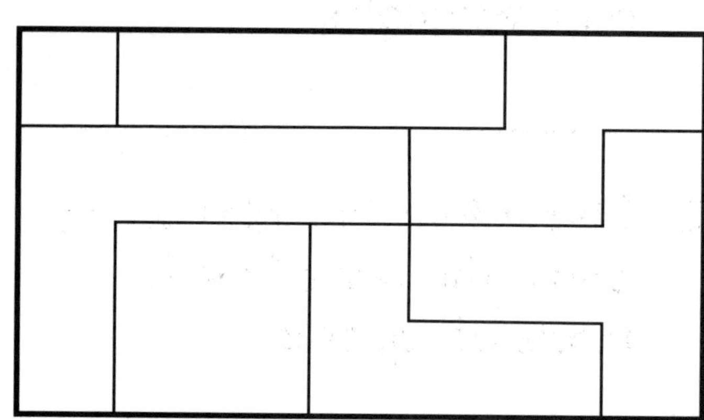

C.

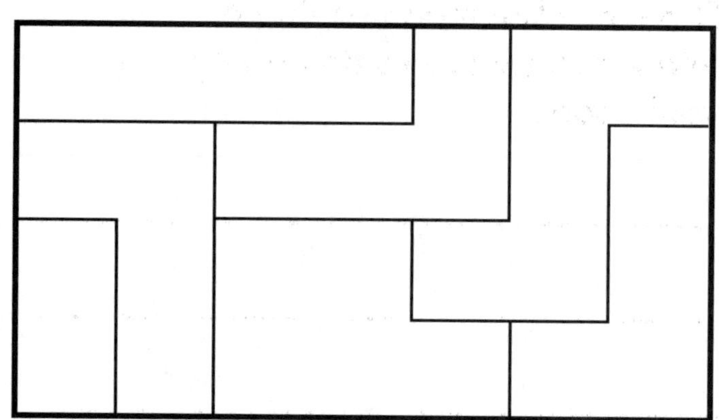

Name ______________________ Date ____________

Find the Robot

Visual Thinking

Read the clues. Write the number of the matching robots.

1. 

2. 

3. 

4. 

A. I have a square head. I am made of squares, circles, and rectangles.

____

B. My head is a rectangle. I have two circles for my feet.

____

C. I have four triangles on my body. The rest of me is made of squares.

____

D. I have two squares for my feet. I have a rectangle for my head.

____

Draw a robot made of shapes. Write two sentences describing your robot.

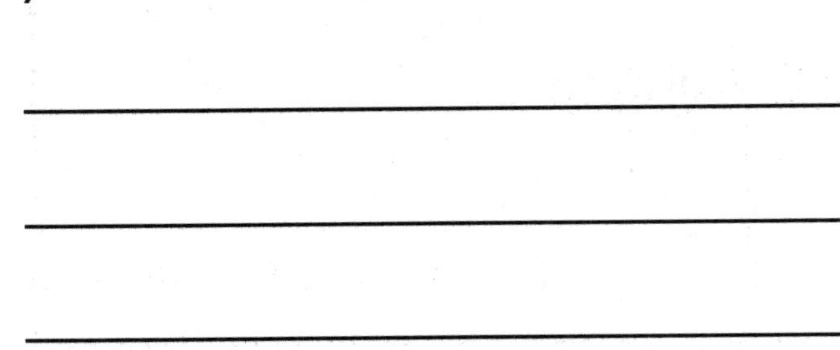

Name ______________________________ Date ______________

Make New Shapes

Visual Thinking

Use a pencil and a ruler to make new shapes.

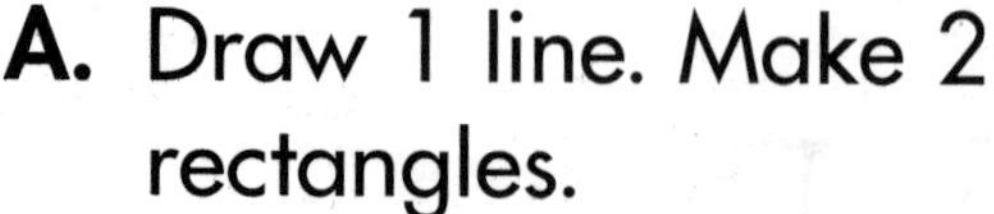

A. Draw 1 line. Make 2 rectangles.

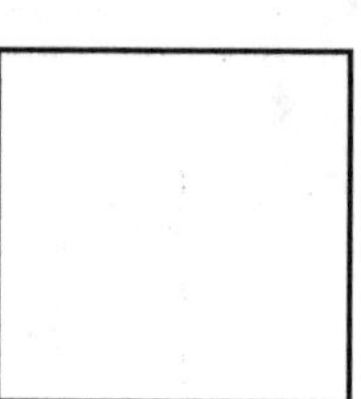

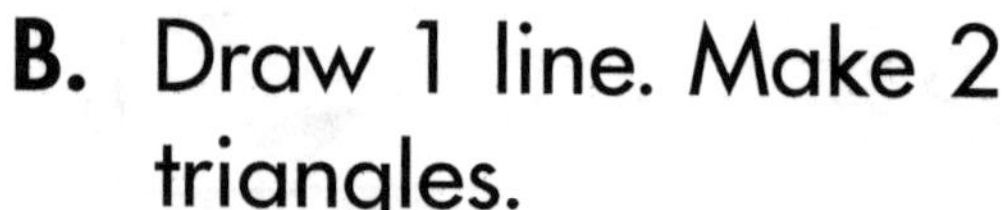

B. Draw 1 line. Make 2 triangles.

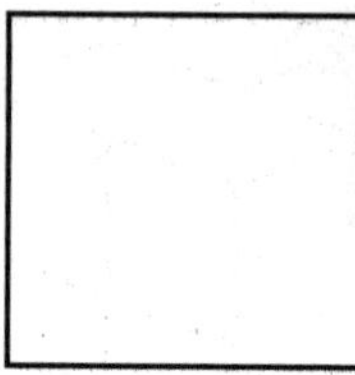

C. Draw 1 line. Make 2 squares.

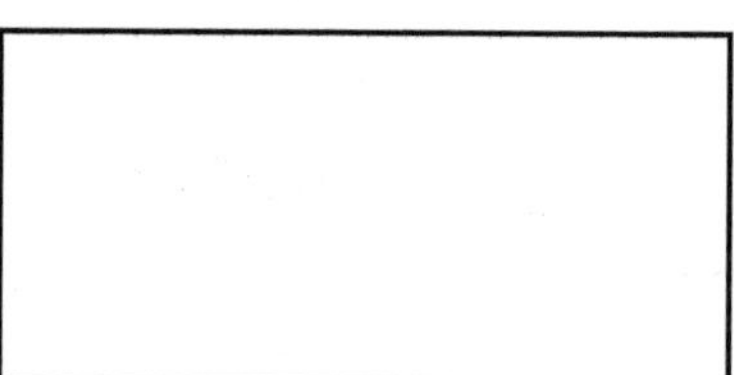

D. Draw 1 line. Make 2 triangles.

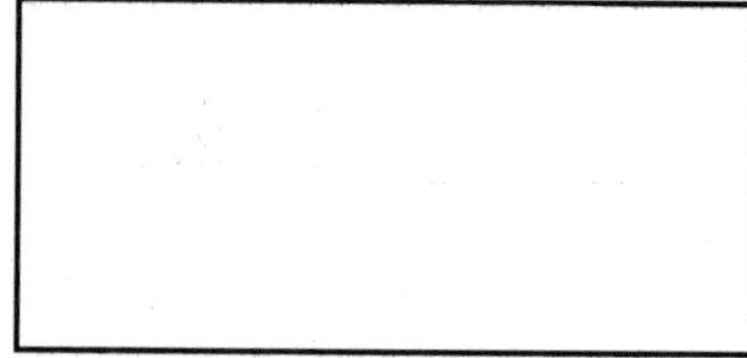

E. Draw 2 lines. Make 4 squares.

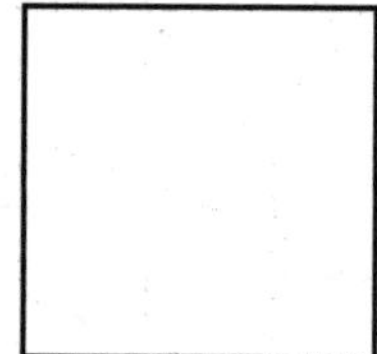

F. Draw 2 lines. Make 3 triangles.

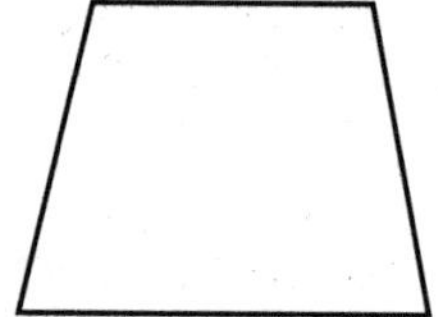

G. Draw 1 line. Make 1 triangle and 1 trapezoid.

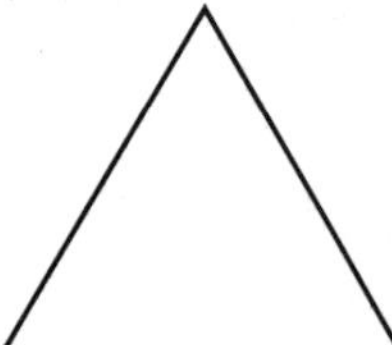

H. Draw 2 lines. Make 3 triangles.

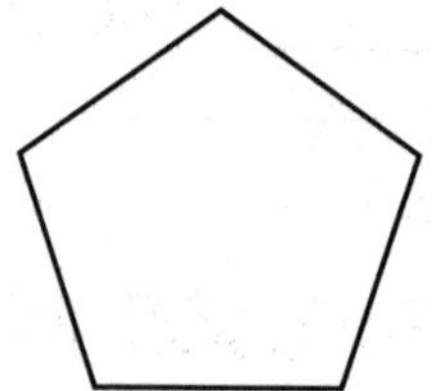

Name ______________________ Date ____________

Block Towers

Visual Thinking

Jerry and Amy made some towers with blocks.

Look at each block tower. Write how many blocks were used to build each tower.

A.

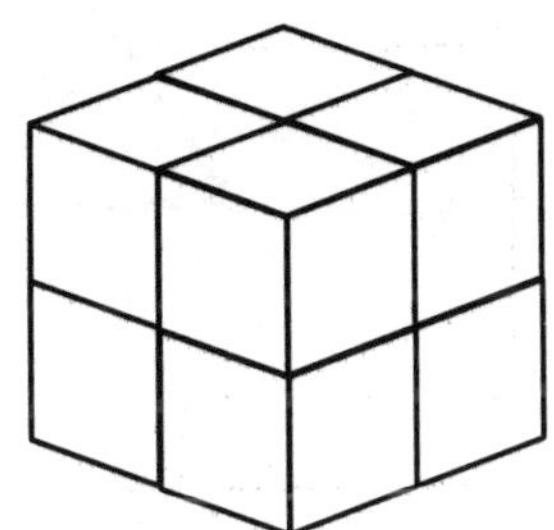

_____ blocks

B.

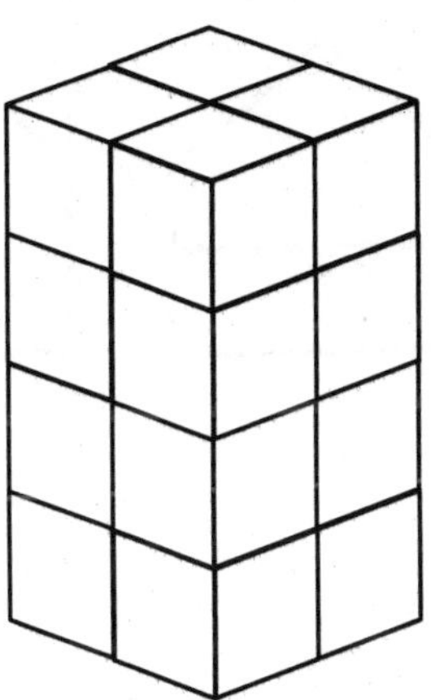

_____ blocks

C.

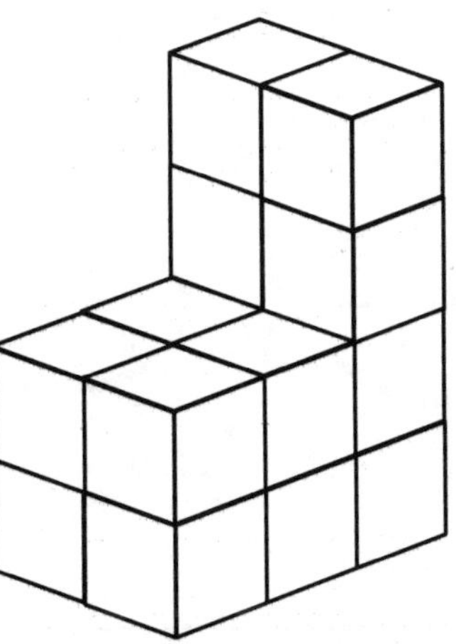

_____ blocks

D.

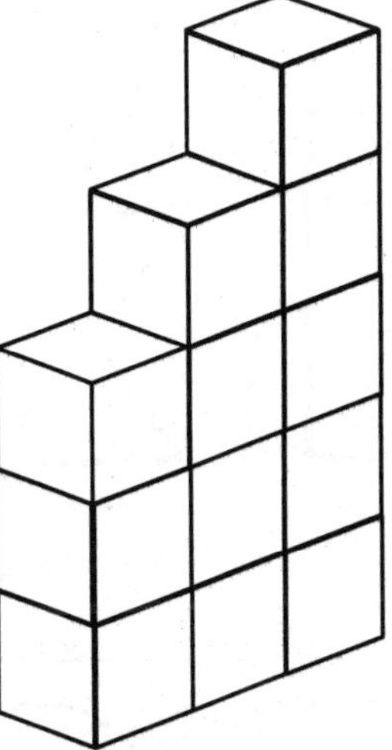

_____ blocks

Which tower used the most blocks? _____

Name ______________________ Date __________

Fold It in Half

Visual Thinking

The dashed line on each shape is a fold line. Suppose you cut out the shapes and folded them on the lines. Circle the number in each pair that shows which shape would be folded so that its halves match exactly.

A.

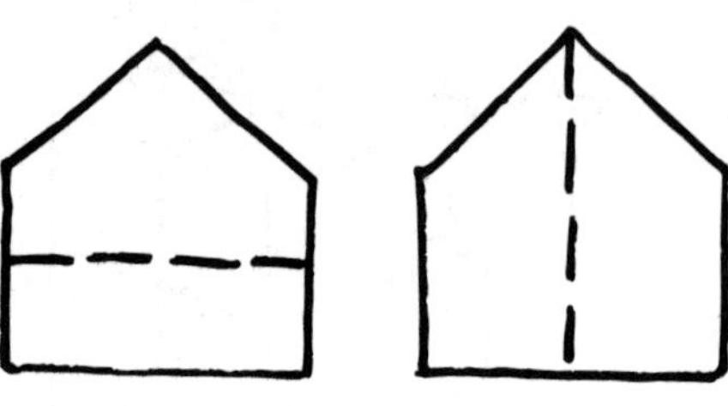

1 2

B.

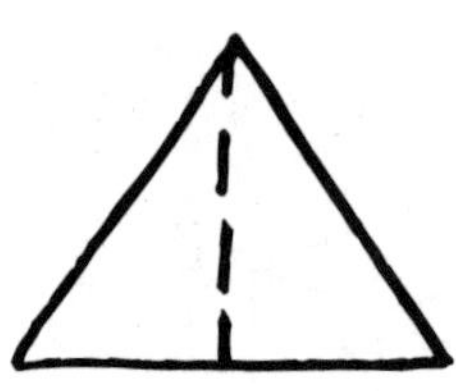

1 2

C.

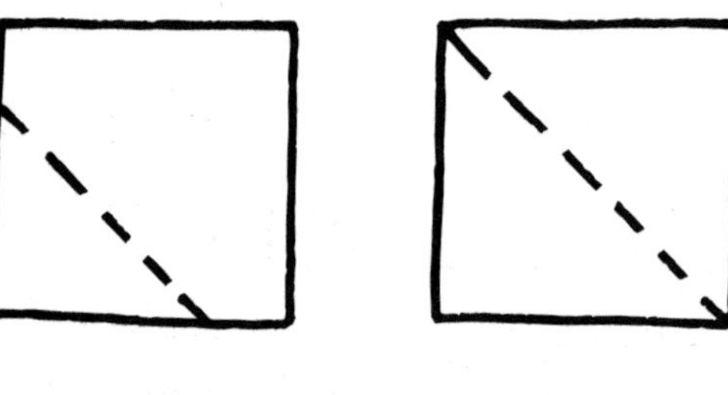

1 2

D.

1 2

E.

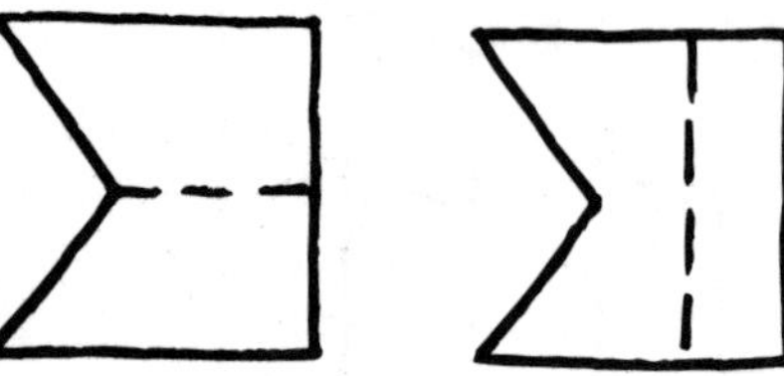

1 2

F.

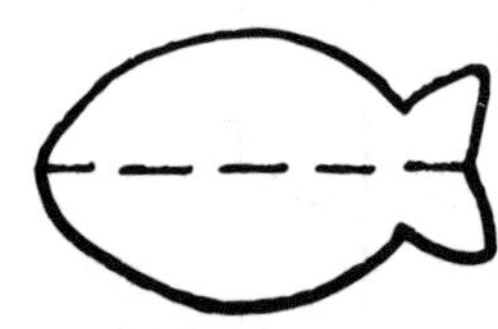

1 2

G.

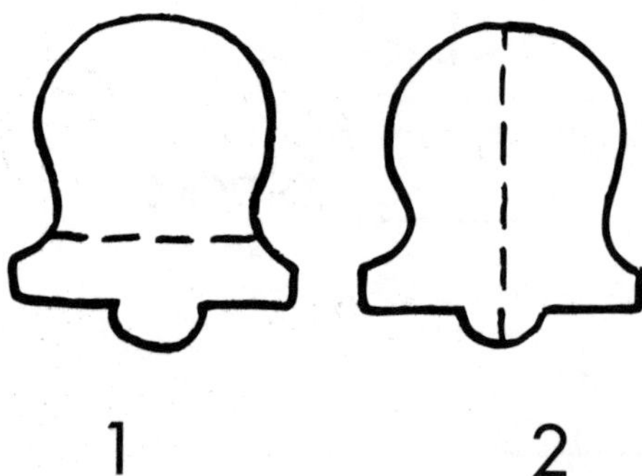

1 2

H.

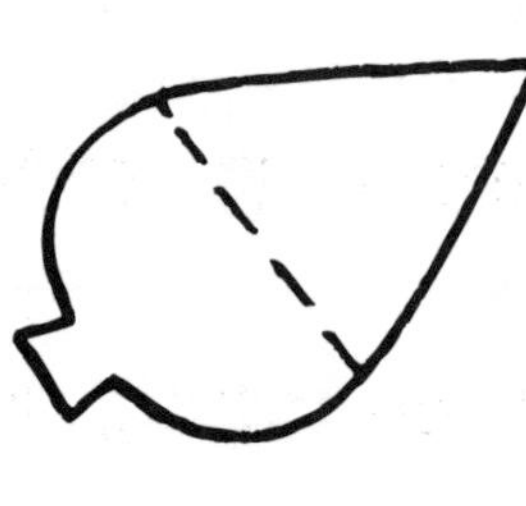

1 2

Name ______________________ Date ____________

Letter Halves

Visual Thinking

Some shapes can be divided in half so that their halves match exactly. These shapes have **symmetry**. The line that divides a shape in half is called the **line of symmetry**.

Draw a line to divide each letter shape into two equal parts.

A.

B.

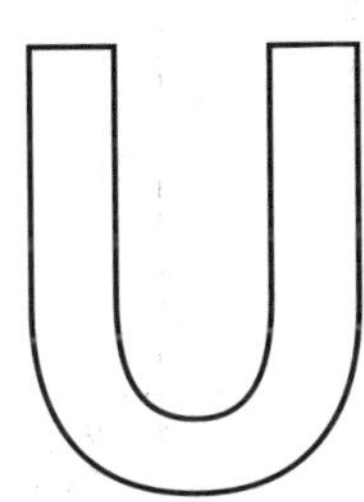

C.

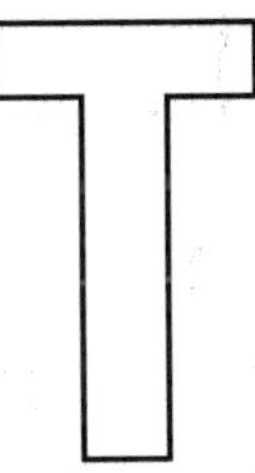

D.

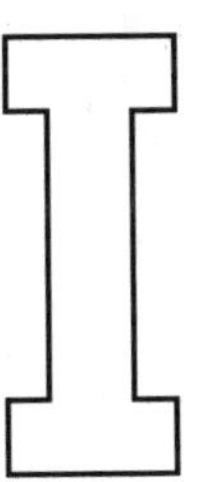

E.

F.

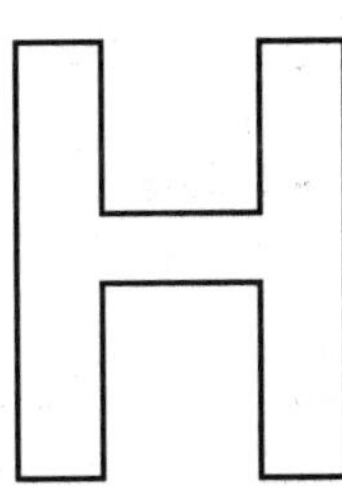

G.

H.

I.

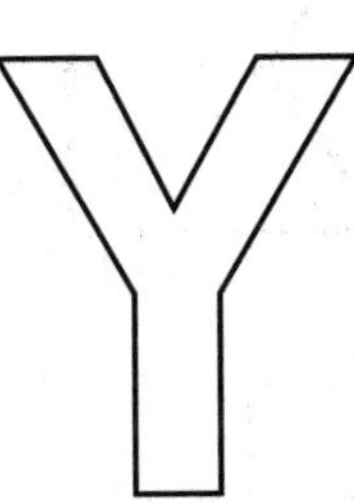

Some letter shapes have two lines of symmetry.

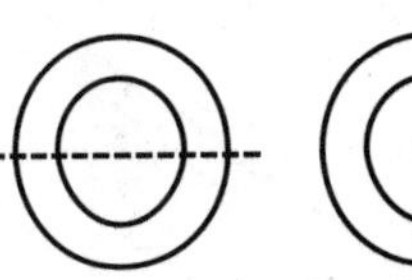

Which letters from above have two lines of symmetry?

____

Name ______________________________ Date ____________

Finish the Halves

Visual Thinking

Finish each shape so that both halves match exactly. The finished shape will then have **symmetry**.

A. B.

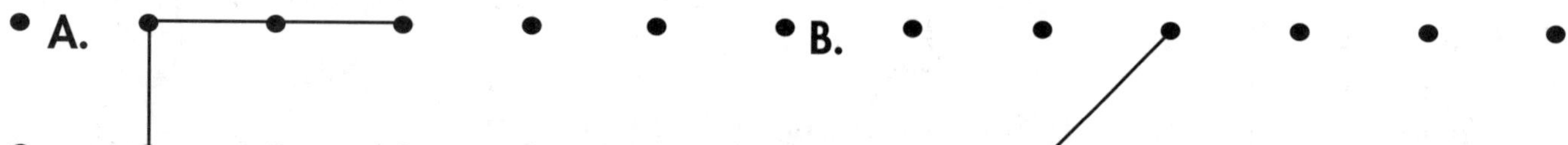

C. D. E.

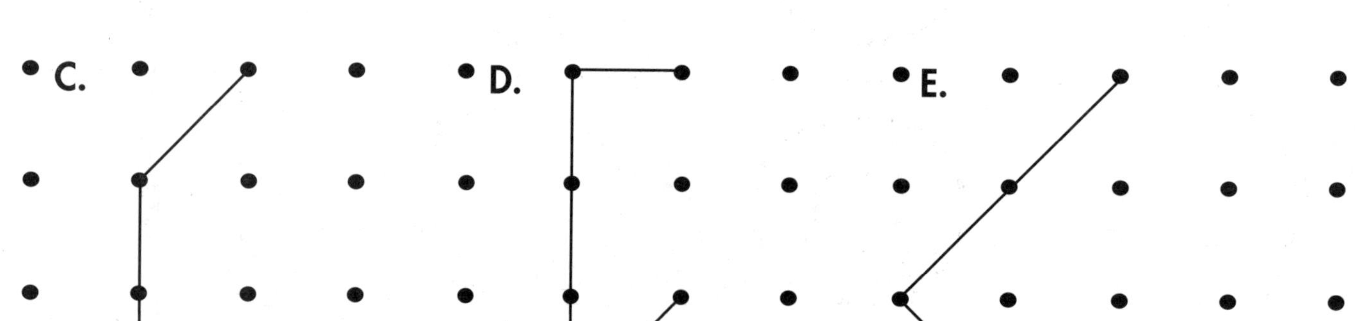

Draw your own symmetrical shape. (If a symmetrical shape is folded in half, both halves will match.)

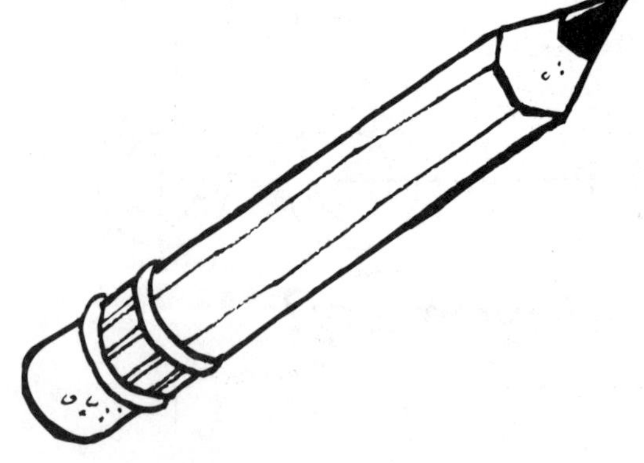

Name ______________________________ Date ______________

Folded Shapes

Visual Thinking

Look at each folded shape. What will the shape look like when it is unfolded? Color its picture.

A. 

B. 

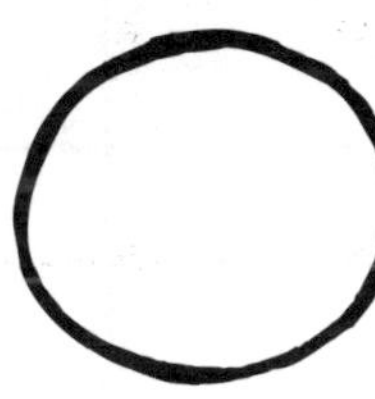  

C. 

  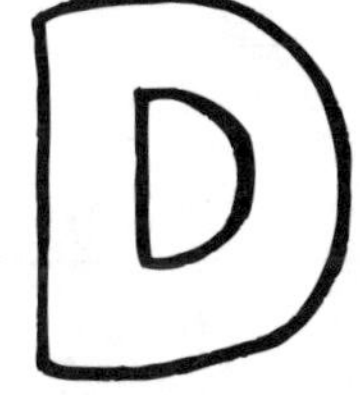

D. 

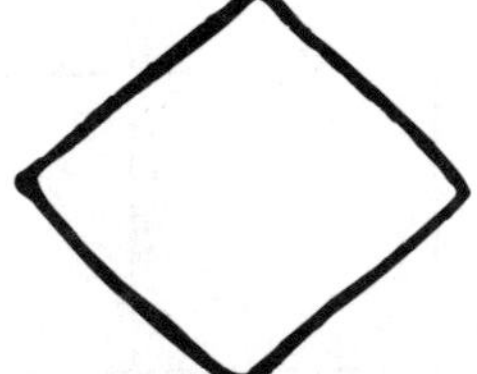  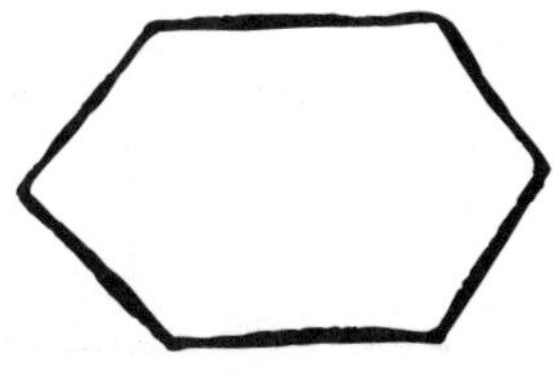

E. 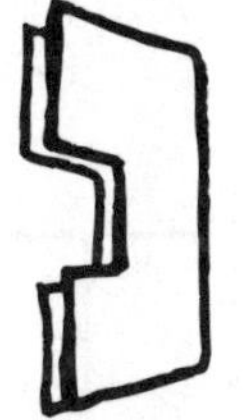

F. 

 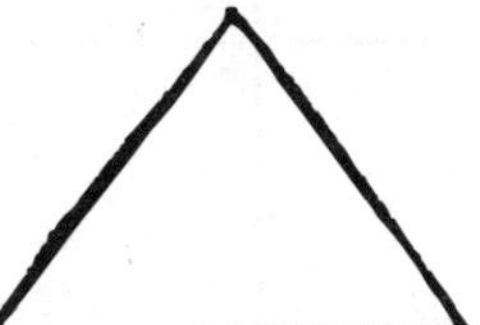 

Name ______________________________ Date ____________

Divide the Rectangle

Visual Thinking

Suppose you can cut the rectangles, but only along the lines shown. How many ways can you cut the rectangle in two equal parts? Use a crayon or marker to show your answers. (You may not need to use all the pictures.)

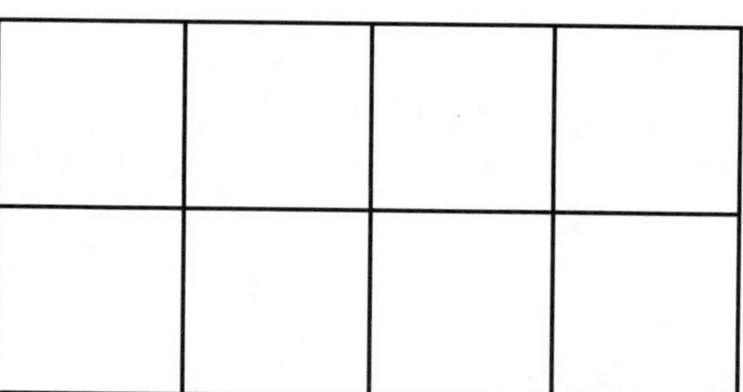

Name ______________________________ Date ______________

Find the Zoo Animals

Use a Picture

Write where each zoo animal can be found. Write the letter and number that tell which two lines the animal is on. The first one is done for you.

A. Where is the  ?

A4

B. Where is the  ?

______

C. Where is the  ?

______

D. Where is the  ?

______

E. Where is the  ?

______

F. Where is the  ?

______

G. Where is the  ?

______

H. Where is the  ?

______

Name ______________________ Date ____________

On the Farm

Logical Thinking

Farmer Fred is looking for his animals. Write where each one can be found. The first one is done for you.

A.  A1

B.  ______

C.  ______

D. ______

E.  ______

F. ______

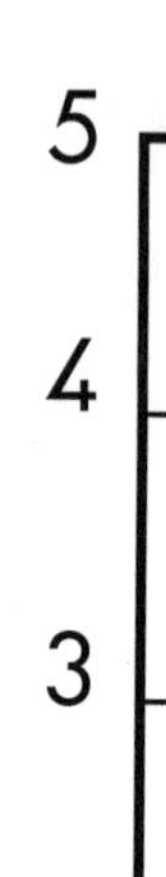

Describe the shortest path from each animal to the farmer. The animals can move up, down, left, and right.

G.  Move 3 spaces to the right. Then move 3 spaces up.

H. ______________________________

I.  ______________________________

Name ______________________________ Date ______________

Show the Time

Logical Thinking

Draw the missing hands on the clocks. Write the times.

One Hour Before | | **One Hour After**

A.

5:00

B.

C.

D.

E.

Name ______________________ Date __________

Ernie's Day

Logical Thinking

Solve each problem. Write the time. Then draw hands on the clock to match.

A. Ernie gets up at 7:00.
He leaves for school one hour later.
What time does Ernie leave for school? _______

B. Ernie's math class starts at 11:00.
The class ends half an hour later.
What time does the math class end? ________

C. Ernie's lunch lasts for half an hour.
Lunch ends at 12:30.
What time does lunch begin? ________

D. Ernie starts his homework at 3:30.
He works for 1 hour and a half.
What time does Ernie finish his homework? _____

E. Ernie goes to Jim's house at 5:30.
He stays there for 2 hours.
What time does Ernie leave Jim's house? _____

F. Ernie reads for half an hour before bedtime.
He goes to bed at 9:00.
What time does Ernie start reading? ________

Name ______________________ Date ____________

Time on the Move

Find and Extend a Pattern

Write the times. Draw hands on the clock to match.

A. One hour later

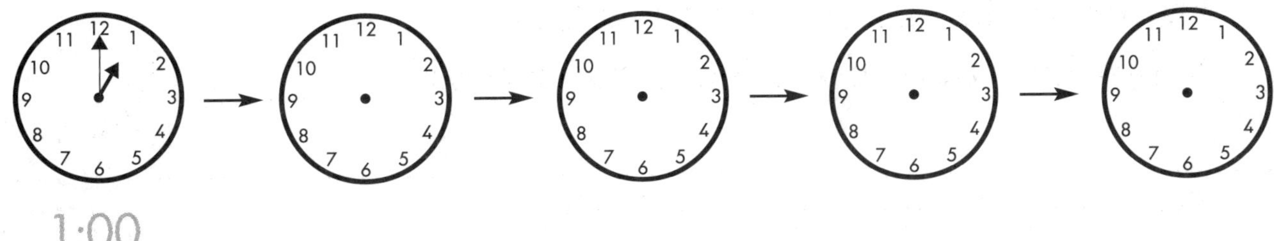

1:00 ______ ______ ______ ______

B. One hour later

______ ______ ______ ______ ______

C. Half an hour later

______ ______ ______ ______ ______

D. Half an hour later

______ ______ ______ ______ ______

Name ______________________________ Date ______________

Passing Time

Find and Extend a Pattern

Write the times. Draw hands on the clocks to match.

A. One hour later

10:15 → ______ → ______ → ______ → ______

B. One hour later

______ → ______ → ______ → ______ → ______

C. Half an hour later

______ → ______ → ______ → ______ → ______

D. Half an hour later

______ → ______ → ______ → ______ → ______

Name ______________________________ Date ____________

Time Puzzlers

Working Backwards

Solve the problems.

A. Neil has a baseball game at 3:00. It will take him half an hour to get to the park. What time does Neil have to leave home to get to the park by 3:00? ____________

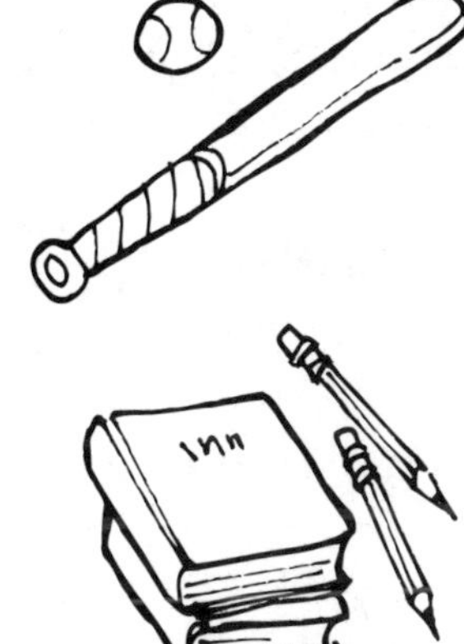

B. Wendy's school starts at 8:30. It takes her 15 minutes to walk to school. What is the latest time that Wendy can leave home?

____

C. A movie ended at 8:00. It lasted 2 hours and a half. What time did the movie start?

____

D. Kenny gets up every morning at 7:00. He always has 10 hours of sleep. What time does Kenny go to bed?

____

E. Jessica shopped for 1 hour and 15 minutes. She finished at 4:15. What time did Jessica start shopping?

____

F. Mickey left his home to visit his grandmother. He stayed for 3 hours and a half. He came home at 1:45 in the afternoon. What time did Kenny leave home? ____________

Name ______________________________ Date ______________

Months of the Year

Use a Diagram

Read the clues. Look at the order of the months.
Then write the month that matches each clue.

A. first month of the year ___January___

B. month after April ______________________

C. month after November ______________________

D. month before July ______________________

E. month before March ______________________

F. third month ______________________

G. tenth month ______________________

H. month after the third month ______________________

I. month before the tenth month ______________________

J. month between June and August ______________________

K. month between October and December ______________________

Write your own clue about the months. Ask someone to write the answer.

____

____

Name ______________________________ Date ____________

Calendar Clues

Use a Diagram

Look at the calendar. Answer the questions.

October						
Sunday	Monday	Tuesday	Wednesday	Thursday	Friday	Saturday
	1	2	3	4	5	6
7	8	9	10	11	12	13
14	15	16	17	18	19	20
21	22	23	24	25	26	27
28	29	30	31			

A. How many days are in October? __________

B. On what day is the first day of the month?

____

C. On what day is the last day of the month?

____

D. What day is October 20? ______________________

E. How many Fridays are in the month? __________

F. What is the date of the second Tuesday of the month?

____

G. Which days occur five times in the month? _______________

____

Name ______________________ Date ____________

How Much Time?

Logical Thinking

Look at each row. Read what the children are saying. Then answer the questions.

A. Ben

Stan

Who will be at camp longer? ____________

B. Tracey

Stacey

Who did their homework faster? ____________

C. Marcie

Joey

Who watched a movie longer? ____________

D. Tom

Terri

Whose birthday will arrive earlier? ____________

Name ______________________________ Date ______________

To the Bear's Cave

Guess and Check

Guess the length of each path in inches.
Write your guess on the chart.
Then measure to check your guess.

______ 1 inch

A.

B.

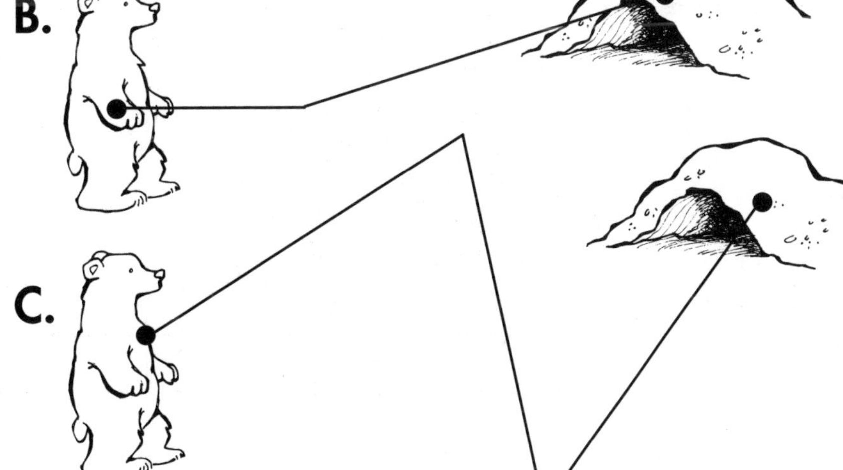

C.

	My Guess (in inches)	My Check (in inches)
A.		
B.		
C.		
D.		
E.		

D.

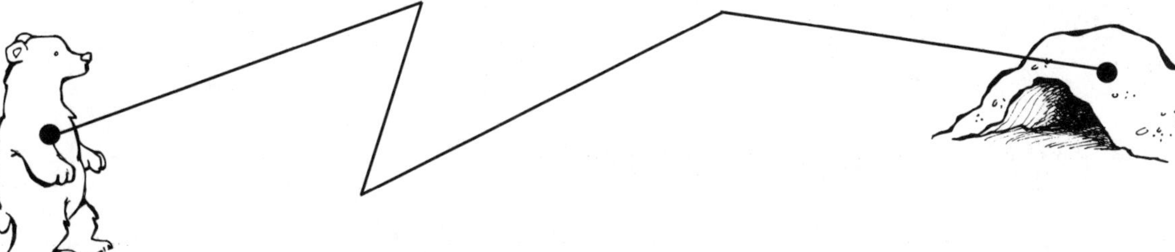

E.

Name ______________________________ Date ______________

Home Sweet Home

Use a Diagram

Use an inch ruler to measure the house. Complete the sentences.

A. The house is _____ inches wide.

B. The side walls are _____ inches high.

C. The door is _____ inches high and _____ inches wide.

D. The window is _____ inches high and _____ inches wide.

E. The highest point of the roof is _____ inches from the ground.

Name ______________________________ Date ____________

Snaky Lengths

Logical Thinking

Mr. Blair's class glued paper ovals together to make snakes.
Read the clues below. Find out how long some of the snakes were.

A. Kathy's snake is 7 inches long.
Mark's snake is 3 inches longer.
Sophie's snake is 2 inches longer than Mark's.
How long are Mark's and Sophie's snakes?

Mark's snake __________ Sophie's snake __________

B. David's snake is 6 inches long.
Kelli's snake is twice as long as David's snake.
Nathan's snake is 3 inches shorter than Kelli's snake.
How long are Kelli's and Nathan's snakes?

Kelli's snake __________ Nathan's snake __________

C. Len's snake is 5 inches.
Ryan's snake is twice as long as Len's snake.
Hannah's snake is twice as long as Ryan's snake.
How long are Ryan's and Hannah's snakes?

Ryan's snake __________ Hannah's snake __________

D. Jeff's snake is 8 inches long.
Mel's snake is 3 inches longer.
Karen's snake is twice as long as Mel's snake.
How long are Mel's and Karen's snakes?

Mel's snake __________ Karen's snake __________

Name ______________________________ Date ______________

Mice and Cheese

Logical Thinking

Help the mice get to the piece of cheese.
First guess the length of each path in centimeters.
Then measure to check your guess. Write the length on the chart.

1 centimeter

My Guess (in centimeters)	My Check (in centimeters)

A. 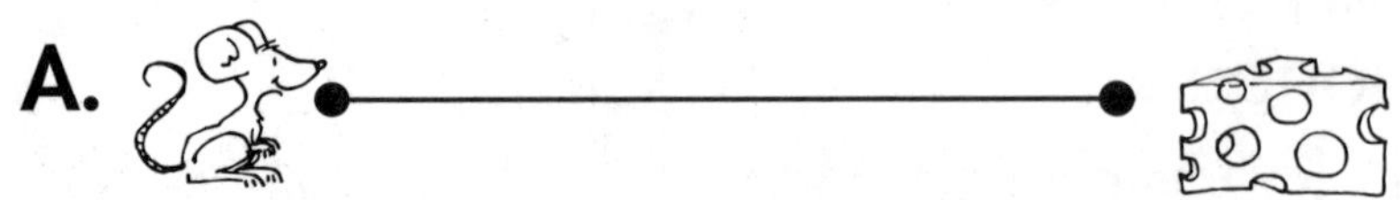

B.

C. 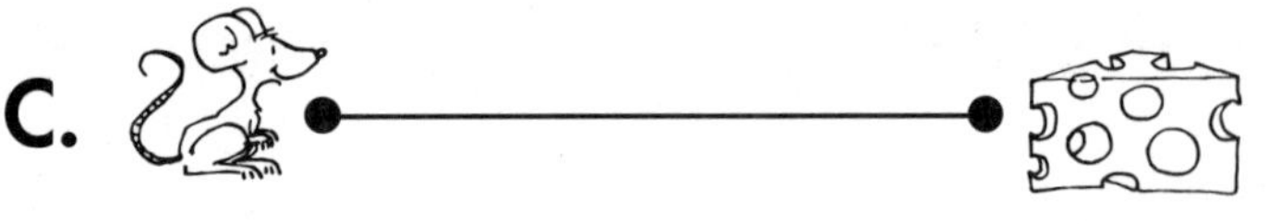

D.

E.

F.  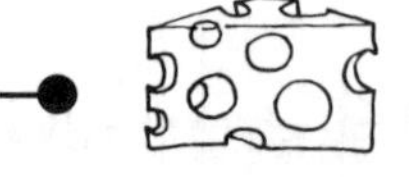

Name ______________________________ Date ______________

On the Go

Guess and Check

Which car took the longest path? Write your guess here. ________
Now check your guess. Measure each car's path with a centimeter ruler.

A.

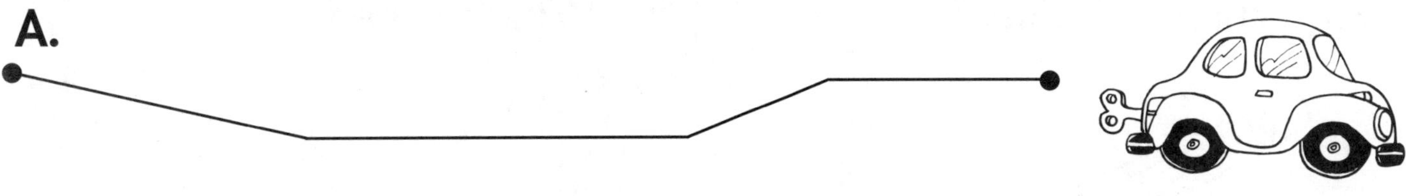

__________ centimeters

B.

__________ centimeters

C.

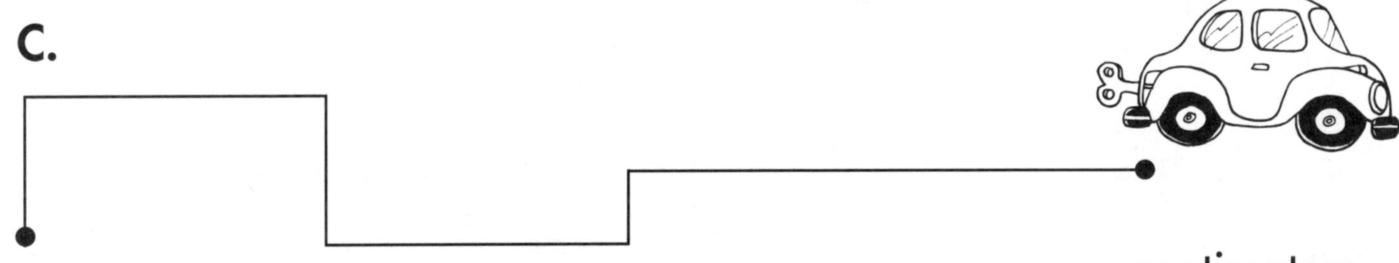

__________ centimeters

D.

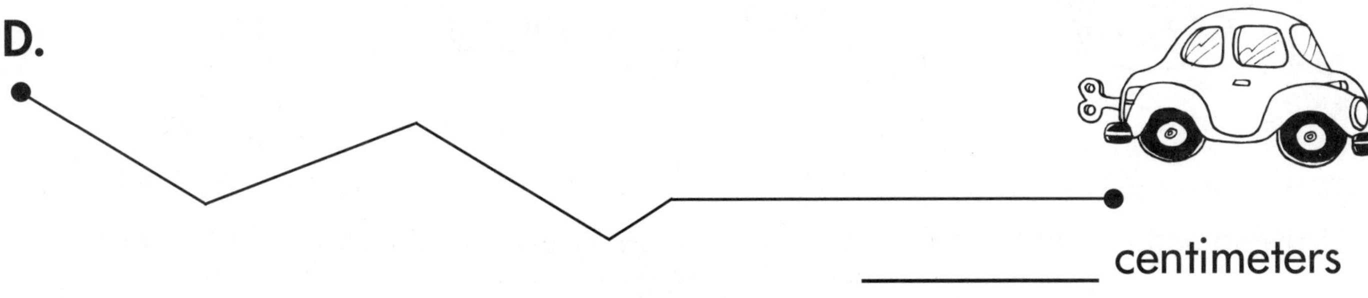

__________ centimeters

Which car took the longest path? _______

Which car took the shortest path? _____

Name ______________________________ Date ______________

Lighter or Heavier?

Logical Thinking

Look at each pair of objects. Circle the object in each pair that answers the question.

A. Which is lighter?

pencil

scissors

B. Which is heavier?

book

eraser

C. Which is heavier?

balloon

basketball

D. Which is lighter?

napkin

cup

E. Which is lighter?

bowl

spoon

F. Which is heavier?

apple

grape

Draw something that is lighter than your shoe. Draw something that is heavier.

lighter

heavier

Name ______________________________ Date ______________

What Do They Weigh?

Logical Thinking

Read the clues. Figure out how much each pet weighs. (All of the cats have the same weight. All of the dogs have the same weight.)

How much does each cat weigh? ________ pounds

How much does each dog weigh? ________ pounds

Draw another picture of the cats and dogs. Show how you can add the weights to get a different sum.

Name ______________________ Date ____________

Pints and Cups

Use a Table, Find and Extend a Pattern

One pint holds the same amount as two cups.

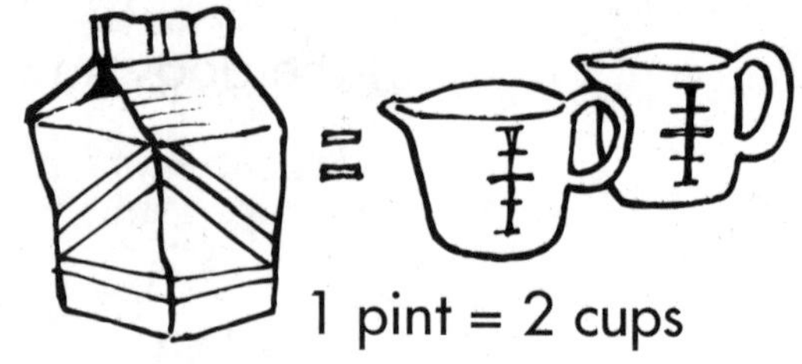

Fill in the chart. Then answer the questions.

1 pint	2 pints	3 pints	___ pints	___ pints	6 pints
2 cups	___ cups	___ cups	8 cups	10 cups	___ cups

A. How many pints equal 4 cups? ____________

B. How many pints equal 8 cups? ____________

C. How many cups equal 3 pints? ____________

D. How many cups equal 5 pints? ____________

E. Which holds more—3 pints or 8 cups? ____________

F. Which holds more—6 pints or 10 cups? ____________

G. How many cups would equal 7 pints? ____________

Name ______________________________ Date ______________

Quarts, Pints, and Cups

Use a Table, Find and Extend a Pattern

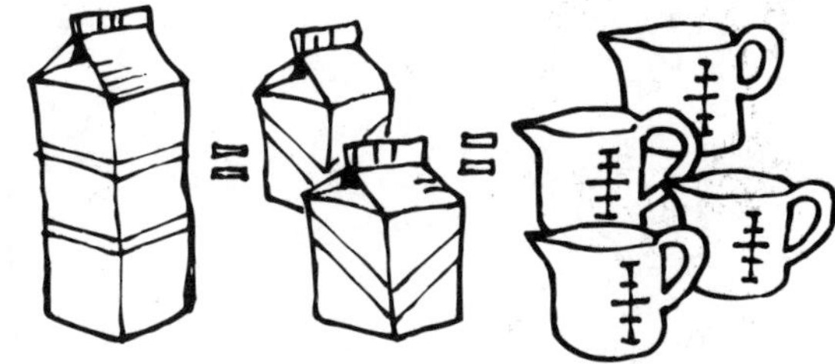

Fill in the chart. Then answer the questions.

1 quart	2 quarts	3 quarts	___ quarts	___ quarts
2 pints	4 pints	___ pints	___ pints	___ pints
4 cups	___ cups	___ cups	16 cups	___ cups

A. How many pints equal 2 quarts? ______________

B. How many cups equal 2 quarts? ______________

C. How many pints equal 5 quarts? ______________

D. How many cups equal 8 pints? ______________

E. How many quarts equal 12 cups? ______________

F. Which holds more—6 pints or 4 quarts? ______________

G. Which holds more—12 cups or 2 quarts? ______________

Name ______________________ Date __________

Fill It Up

Use a Picture, Logical Thinking

2 cups = 1 pint

2 pints = 1 quart

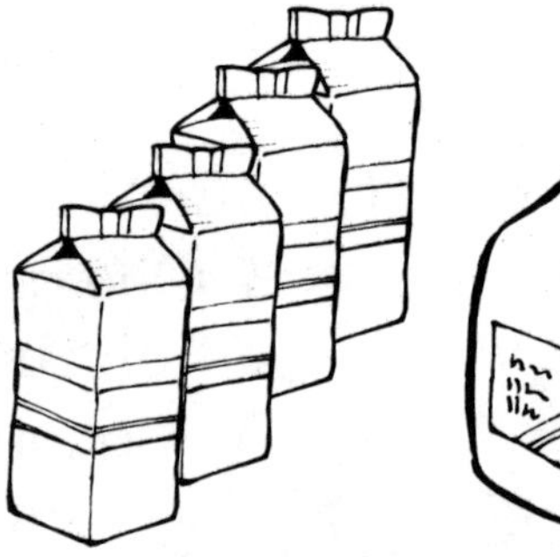

4 quarts = 1 gallon

Which holds more? Circle the pictures to show your answers.

A. 2 cups or 2 pints

B. 3 cups or 1 quart

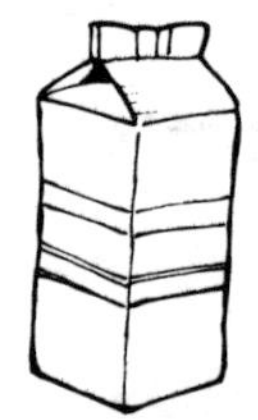

C. 6 pints or 2 quarts

D. 2 quarts or 1 gallon

E. 5 quarts or 1 gallon

F. 6 cups or 1 quart

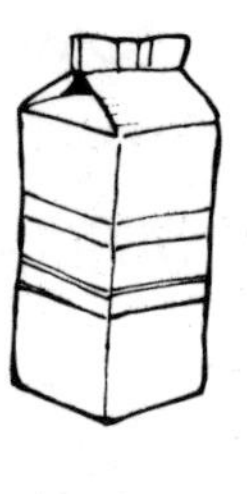

Name ______________________________ Date ______________

Taking Up Space

Use a Picture

Look at the shapes on the grid.
Count the squares to find out how much space each shape takes up.
Write the number of squares on the lines.

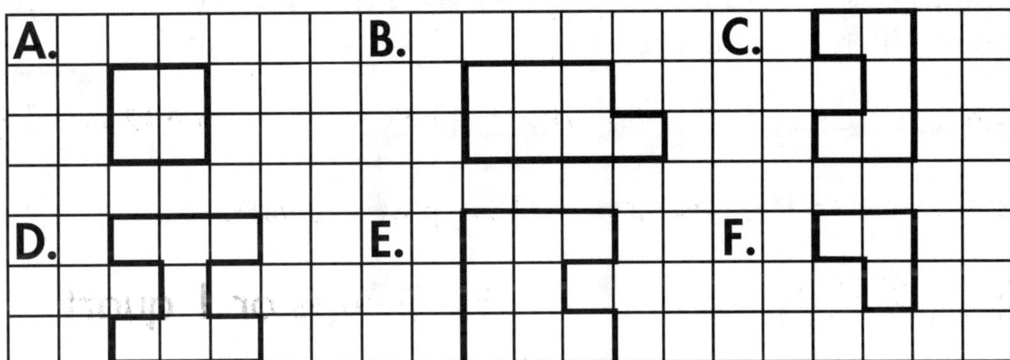

A. ______ squares **B.** ______ squares **C.** ______ squares

D. ______ squares **E.** ______ squares **F.** ______ squares

G. Which shape took up the most space? Write its letter. _____

H. Which shape took up the least amount of space? Write its letter. _____

I. Which two shapes took up the same amount of space?

____

In the grid at the right, draw two different shapes that take up the same amount of space.

Name ________________________________ Date ______________

Floor Tiles

Draw a Diagram

Mr. Lee works with square tiles.
He uses the tiles to cover floors.
How many tiles does he need for each floor below?
To find out, get a ruler and a pencil. Connect the dots to make squares. Then count the squares.

A. 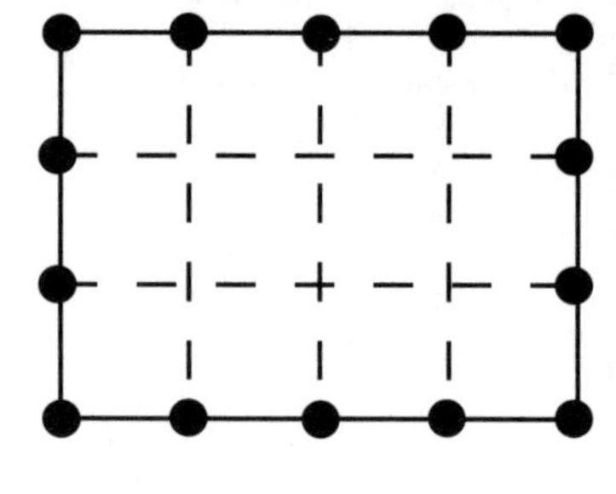

_____ tiles

B. 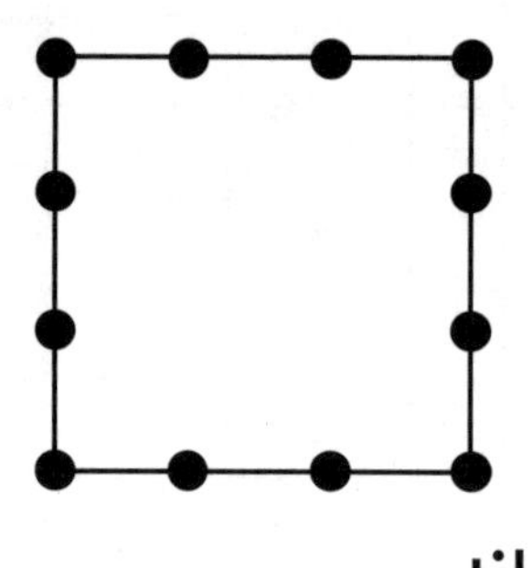

_____ tiles

C. 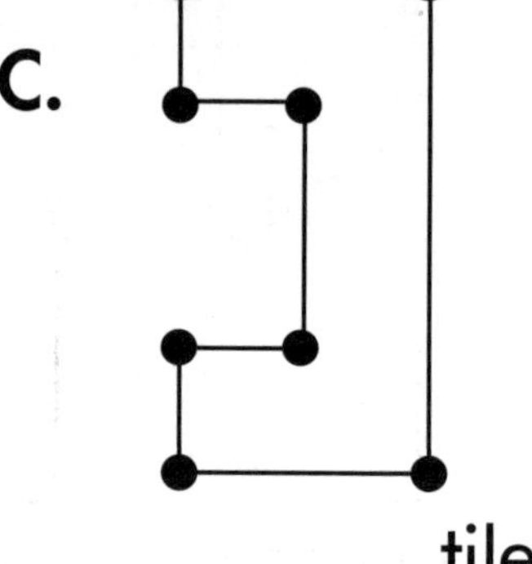

_____ tiles

D. 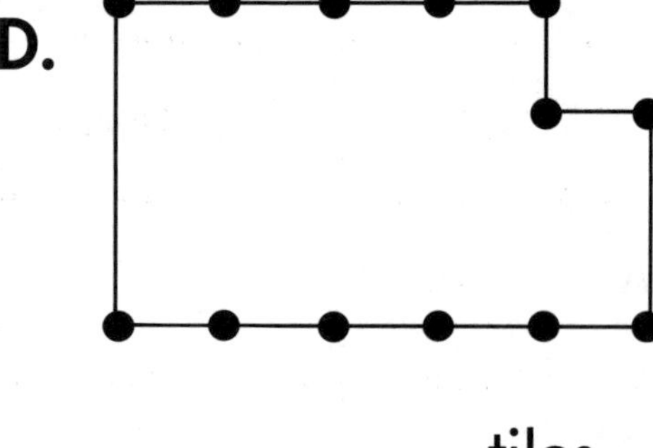

_____ tiles

E. 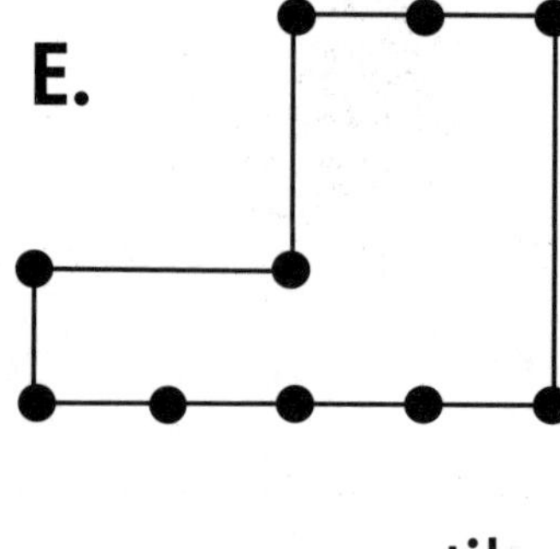

_____ tiles

F. 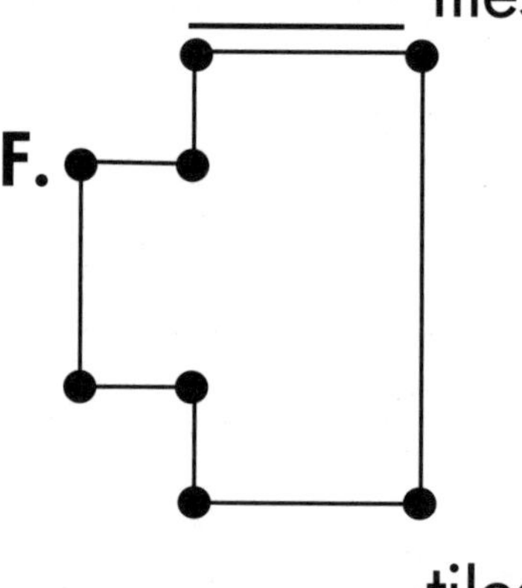

_____ tiles

G. Which floor took up the most space? _____

H. Which floor took up the least amount of space? _____

I. How many more tiles does floor B need than floor E? _____

J. How many more tiles does floor A need than floor F? _____

Name ______________________________ Date ______________

Starry Problems

Collecting and Interpreting Information

Make tally marks to count the stars. Then fill in the chart.

	Tally	Number
Stars in the circle only		
Stars in the rectangle only		
Stars in the triangle only		
Stars in both the triangle and rectangle		
Stars in both the rectangle and circle		
Total number of stars		

Name ______________________________ Date ______________

Hunting for Bones

Collecting and Interpreting Information

Help Sparky find his bones.
Make tally marks to count the bones.
Then fill in the chart.

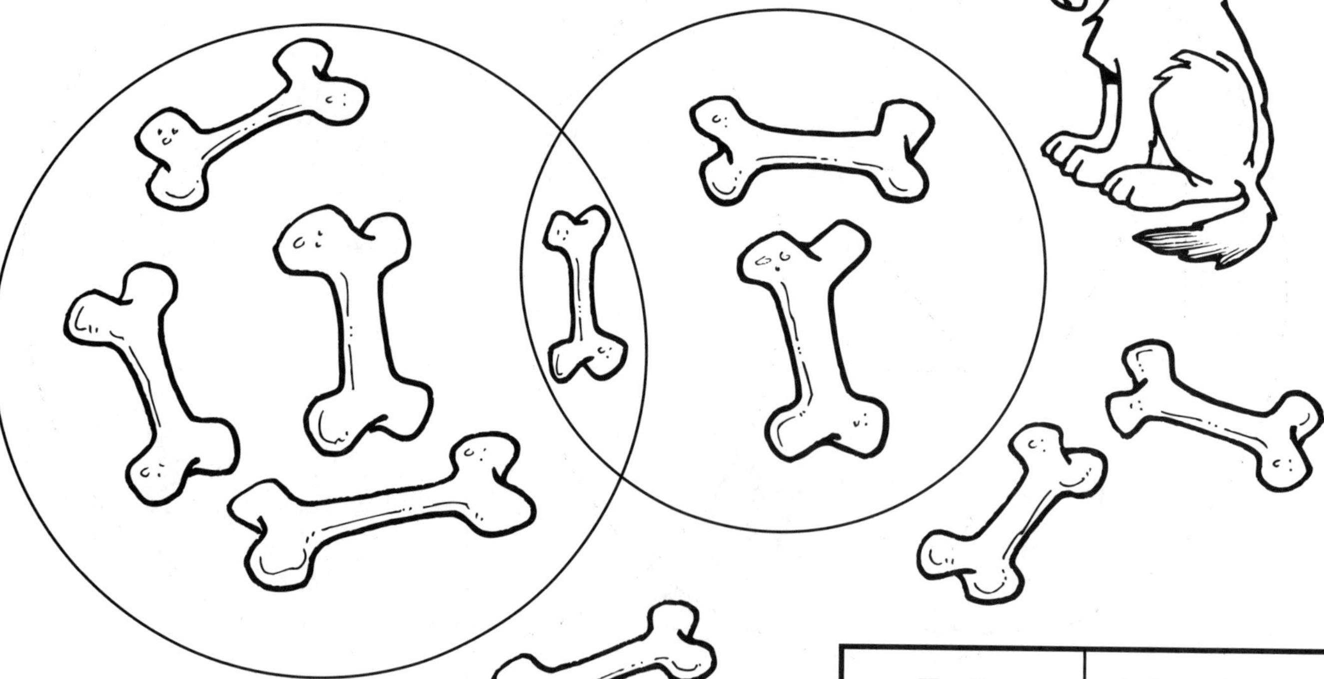

	Tally	Number
Bones in the small circle only		
Bones in the large circle only		
Bones in both the large circle and the small circle		
Bones not in a circle		
Total number of bones		

Name ____________________ Date ____________

Sorting Shapes

Interpreting information

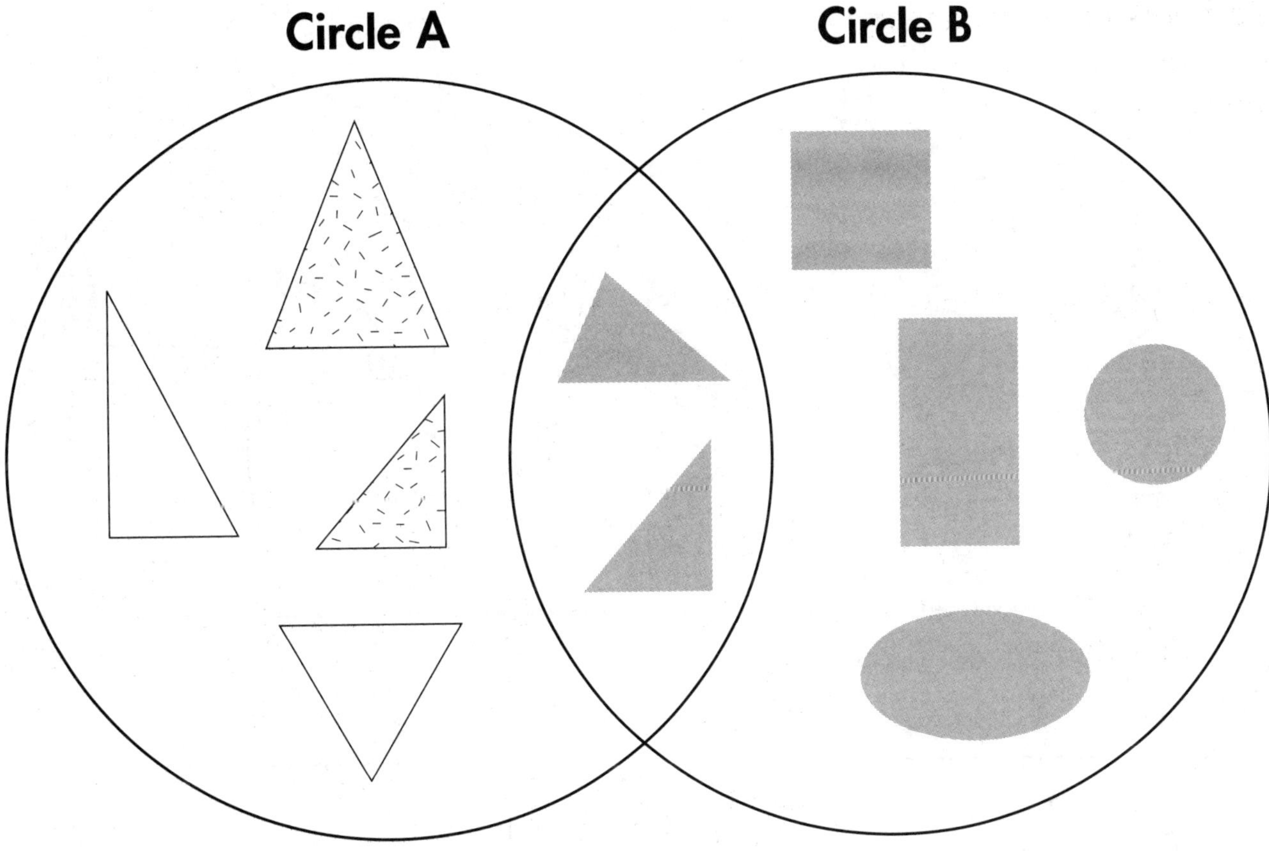

A. Look at the shapes in circle A. What is the same?

____

B. Look at the shapes in circle B. What is the same?

____

C. How can you describe the shapes in both circles?

____

D. Draw another shape that can go in both circles.

Name ______________________________ Date ______________

Under the Sea

Collecting and Interpreting Information

Count the sea animals. Draw tally marks to show how many you find.

Use your tally marks to help you answer the questions.

A. How many  are there? ________

B. How many  are there? ________

C. How many  are there? ________

D. How many more  are there than 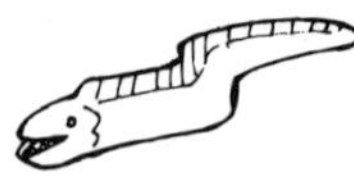 ? ________

E. How many sea animals are there in all? ________

Name ______________________________ Date ______________

Favorite Pets

Interpreting Information

Miss Martin asked her students to name the animal they would most like for a pet. She made a tally chart to show which animals they picked.

Favorite Animals

Animal	Tally
dog	卌 ||
cat	卌 |
 fish	|||
 mouse	||||
 hamster	卌

A. How many students liked cats the best? ________

B. How many students liked hamsters the best? ________

C. Which animal was picked by the most number of students?

____

D. Which animal was picked by the least number of students?

____

E. Did more students pick cats or mice? ______________

F. How many students are in Miss Martin's class? ________

Name ______________________________ Date ____________

Baby Bunnies

Collecting and Interpreting Information

Color the graph to show how many bunnies each child has.

Bert							
Kris							
Mike							
Pam							
Jake							
	1	2	3	4	5	6	7

Use the graph to answer the questions.

A. Who has the most bunnies? ____________

B. Who has the least number of bunnies? ____________

C. Who has three more bunnies than Jake? ____________

D. Who has three more bunnies than Bert? ____________

E. How many bunnies are there in all? ____________

Name ______________________ Date ____________

Favorite Places

Collecting and Interpreting Information

Mr. Curtis asked his students to vote for their favorite places. He made a tally chart to show how they voted.

Favorite Places	
Zoo	~~||||~~ ||
Park	~~||||~~ ||||
Library	~~||||~~
Museum	|||

Use the tally chart to make a bar graph. Color one box for every tally.

Zoo										
Park										
Library										
Museum										
	1	2	3	4	5	6	7	8	9	10

Which place got the most votes? ____________

Which place got the least votes? ____________

Name ______________________________ Date ____________

How Tall?

Interpreting information

The five Turner children grew some bean plants. They measured the heights of their plants. Then they made a bar graph to show the different heights.

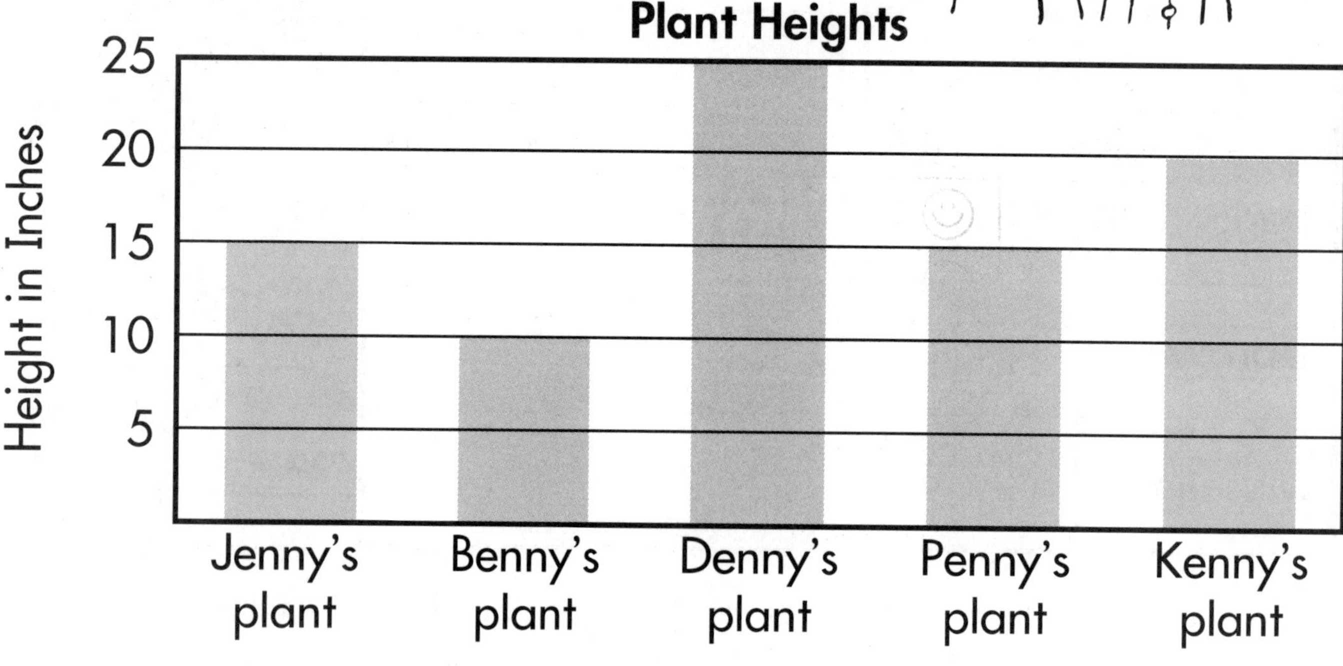

A. How tall is Jenny's plant? ______________

B. Whose plant is the tallest? ______________

C. Whose plant is the shortest? ______________

D. Whose two plants are the same height?

____

E. Whose plant is taller than Penny's plant, but shorter than Denny's plant? ______________

Name ____________________ Date ____________

A Juicy Graph

Interpreting Information

Laura asked her friends to name their favorite kind of drink. The picture graph shows their answers.

Favorite Drinks	
Apple Juice	☺ ☺ ☺ ☺ ☺ ☺
Orange Juice	☺ ☺ ☺ ☺
Grape Juice	☺ ☺
Fruit Punch	☺ ☺ ☺ ☺ ☺
Lemonade	☺ ☺ ☺

☺ = 1 child

Use the graph to answer the questions.

A. How many children chose orange juice? ____________

B. How many children chose lemonade? ____________

C. Which juice was chosen the most often? ____________

D. Which juice was chosen the least often? ____________

E. How many children chose fruit punch or grape juice?

____

F. How many children chose apple juice or orange juice?

____

G. How many children did Laura ask in all? ____________

Name ______________________ Date ____________

Butterfly Hunt

Interpreting Information

Tina and Sam like to look for butterflies.
They made a chart showing how many butterflies they counted on the weekend.

Number of Butterflies	
Friday	
Saturday	
Sunday	

 = 2 butterflies

A. How many butterflies did the children see on Friday?

____

B. How many butterflies did the children see on Saturday?

____

C. How many butterflies did the children see on Sunday?

____

D. How many more butterflies did they see on Sunday than on Friday? ____________

E. How many more butterflies did they see on Saturday than on Sunday? ____________

F. How many butterflies did they see in all? ____________

Name ______________________________ Date ______________

Pick a Cube

Probability

Look at the cubes on this page.
Color five cubes purple, two cubes orange, and one cube yellow.

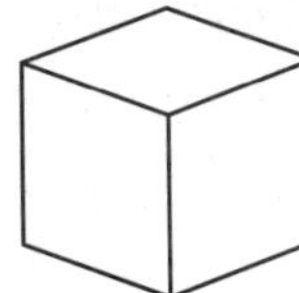

Suppose you put the cubes in a bag.
Pretend you are going to close your eyes and take out a cube.
Then answer the questions.

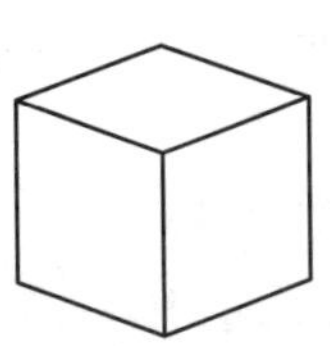

A. What color cube will you most likely take out of the bag? ______________

Why? ______________

____

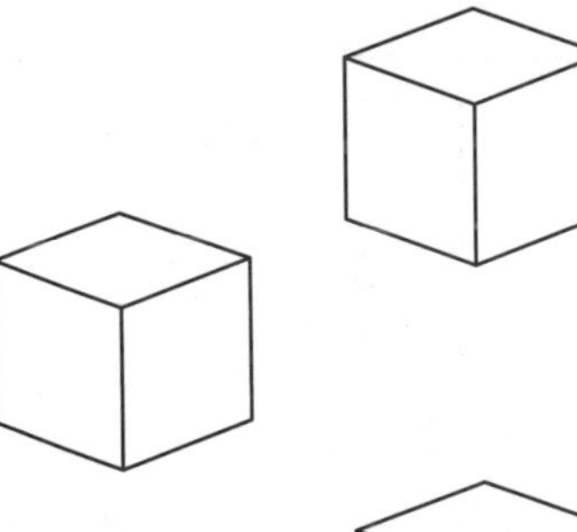

B. What color cube will you least likely take out of the bag? ______________

Why? ______________

____

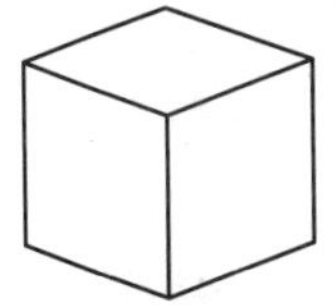

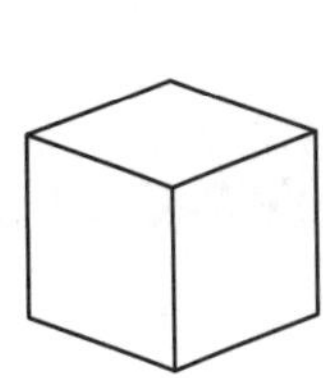

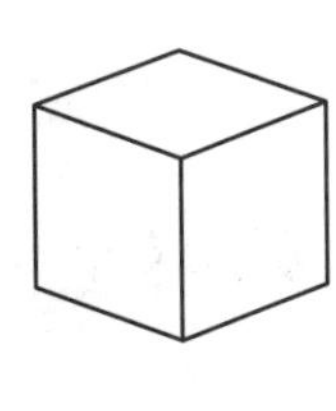

C. Suppose you got a second bag.
Which cubes would you put in the bag so that you have the same chance of getting a purple cube, an orange cube, and a yellow cube? Explain your answer.

____

____

Name ______________________________ Date ____________

Andy's Socks

Probability

Use the code to color Andy's socks.

Code
b—blue
r—red
y—yellow

Andy put the socks in a basket for a game. He is going to close his eyes and pick a sock. Answer the questions to tell what his chances are of picking a certain color.

A. Is it more likely or less likely that Andy will get a red sock?

____

B. Is it more likely or less likely that Andy will pick a yellow sock?

____

C. Does he have a better chance of picking a blue sock or a yellow sock?

____

D. Which color does Andy have the least chance of picking?

____

E. Which color does Andy have the best chance of picking?

____

Name ______________________________ Date ______________

A Flag Maker

Organize Information, Use a Picture

Mrs. Flagler sews colorful flags for children.
She uses blue, purple, or green cloth for the flags.
She uses red or yellow cloth for the stars in each flag.
Color the flags to show the different flags Mrs. Flagler can make.

Name ______________________________ Date ______________

Pairs of Fish

Organize Information, Use a Picture

Robbie's dad said that he can buy two goldfish. The goldfish are red, yellow, and orange. He can buy two fish of the same color or two fish of different colors. Color the fish to show the different pairs Robbie can choose from.

Name ______________________________ Date ______________

Mr. Drake's Ducks

Organize Information, Use a Picture

Mr. Drake sells toy ducks for a hobby.
He paints the ducks yellow, orange, or brown.
He adds in a bow that is red, purple, or blue.
Color the ducks to show the different ways
Mr. Drake can pair up the colors.

Answer Key

How Many Beads? (page 5)

A. 3
B. 2
C. 4
D. 3
E. 5
F. 2

Super Sums (page 6)

Answers will vary. Possible answers include:
A. 3 + 5 + 7 = 15
B. 9 + 4 + 2 = 15
C. 1 + 6 + 8 = 15
D. 4 + 5 + 6 = 15
E. 1 + 2 + 4 + 8 = 15
F. 3 + 5 + 1 + 6 = 15
Tip: Students may wish to put 15 counters into groups to create their number sentences.

Hidden Sums (page 7)

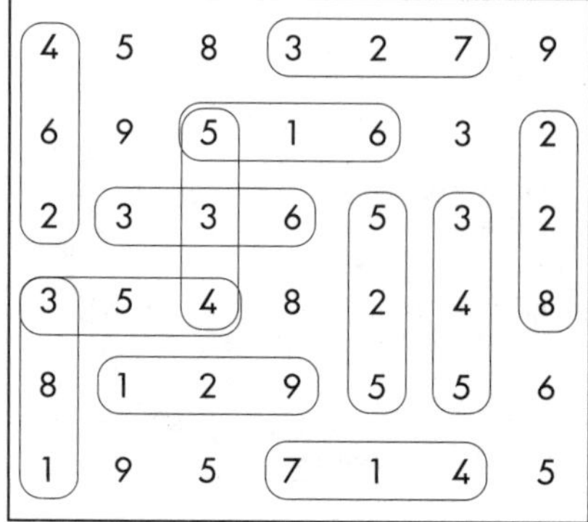

Plus and Minus Puzzler (page 8)

A. 3 + 5 = 9 − 1
B. 6 − 4 = 8 − 6
C. 10 − 5 = 2 + 3
D. 6 + 6 = 9 + 3
E. 11 − 2 = 3 + 6
F. 7 + 3 = 2 + 8
G. 11 − 4 = 12 − 5
H. 8 + 5 = 7 + 6
I. 5 + 3 = 10 − 2
J. 13 − 5 = 6 + 2
K. 10 − 6 = 12 − 8
L. 12 − 3 = 4 + 5

Students' problems will vary.

Plus and Minus Challenge (page 9)

A. 4 + 3 − 1 = 5 + 5 − 4
B. 2 + 6 + 1 = 7 + 3 − 1
C. 10 − 2 − 3 = 1 + 2 + 2
D. 6 + 5 − 3 = 7 + 3 − 2
E. 9 − 2 + 5 = 4 + 4 + 4
F. 3 + 6 + 2 = 8 + 4 − 1
G. 7 + 7 − 5 = 6 + 6 − 3
H. 8 − 3 + 9 = 12 − 4 + 6
I. 13 − 5 + 7 = 5 + 5 + 5
J. 5 + 6 − 4 = 12 − 7 + 2

Waiting in Line (page 10)

A. 6
B. 3
C. 5
D. 3
E. 5
F. 4
G. Susie, Cory, Alex, Jan, Dana, Max, Brett, Lisa

Who Am I? (page 11)

A. Evan
B. Rachel
C. Ricky
D. Stacy
E. Max
F. Lori

On the Bus (page 12)

A. 6 − 2 + 1 = **5** people
B. 7 − 4 + 3 = **6** people
C. 10 + 2 + 2 + 2 = **16** people
D. 15 − 4 − 4 = **7** people
E. 5 + 6 = 11
15 − 11 = **4** students
F. 12 − 5 = 7
14 − 7 = **7** boy scouts
Tip: Students may wish to find the solutions by acting out the problems, using counters, or drawing pictures.

Mystery Numbers (page 13)

A. 36
B. 89
C. 62
D. 64
E. 28
F. 91
G. 49

Adding Odd and Even Numbers (page 14)

A. even; 18, 56, 58
B. even; 12, 46, 88
C. odd; 19, 67, 93
D. When you add two even numbers, you get an even answer.
E. When you add two odd numbers, you get an even answer.
F. When you add an odd number and an even number, you get an odd answer.

Subtracting Odd and Even Numbers (page 15)

A. even; 6, 4, 12
B. even; 4, 20, 62
C. odd; 13, 41, 37
D. When you subtract an even number from an even number, you get an even answer.
E. When you subtract an odd number from an odd number, you get an even answer.
F. When you subtract an even number from an odd number or an odd number from an even

number, you get an odd answer.

Addition Mysteries (page 16)

43 + 14 = 57
17 + 32 = 49
56 + 31 = 87
41 + 57 = 98
69 + 13 = 82
27 + 59 = 86
68 + 30 = 98
34 + 56 = 90

Subtraction Mysteries (page 17)

75 − 32 = 43
54 − 24 = 30
97 − 41 = 56
89 − 67 = 22
78 − 18 = 60
60 − 18 = 42
57 − 18 = 39
93 − 75 = 18

Bug Watch (page 18)

A. 65 − 24 = 41; **41** bees
B. 30 + 48 = 78; **78** ants
C. 21 + 15 = 36; **36** butterflies
D. 28 − 11 = 17; **17** flies
E. 54 + 45 = 99; **99** beetles
F. 36 − 31 = 5; **5** ladybugs
G. 47 − 20 = 27; **27** caterpillars
H. 41 + 27 = 68; **68** moths

Sticker Fun (page 19)

A. 40 car stickers
B. 70 dog stickers
C. 8 silver stars
D. 42 gold stars

Guess Benny's Number (page 20)

75

Guess Jenny's Number (page 21)

46

Number Trios (page 22)

A. 123, 132, 213, 231, 312, 321
B. 456, 465, 546, 564, 645, 654
C. 789, 798, 879, 897, 978, 987

Hocus, Pocus! (page 23)

A. 953, 359, 593
B. 641, 146, 416
C. 872, 278, 827

Book Talk (page 24)

A. 50 + 62 = 112; **112** books
B. 45 + 35 = 80; 150 − 80 = 70; **70** pages
C. 24 + 43 + 38 = 105; **105** books
D. 16 + 8 + 4 = 28; **28** books

Fun at the Fair (page 25)

A. 320 + 425 = 745; **745** people
B. 270 − 150 = 120; **120** balloons
C. 100 − 29 = 71; **71** teddy bears
D. 175 − 96 = 79; **79** bags of popcorn
E. 39 + 14 + 48 = 101; **101** pies
F. 190 − 95 = 95; **95** people
G. 184 − 36 = 148; **148** people

Making Cents (page 26)

Answers will vary. Possible answers include:
1 quarter, 2 dimes, 1 nickel
4 dimes, 2 nickels
1 quarter, 5 nickels
10 nickels
1 quarter, 2 dimes, 5 pennies

What's in the Bag? (page 27)

A. 1 dime, 1 nickel
B. 1 quarter, 1 dime
C. 1 quarter, 2 dimes
D. 2 dimes, 1 nickel
E. 2 quarters, 1 dime
F. 2 quarters, 2 nickels
G. 3 quarters, 1 dime
H. 2 quarters, 3 nickels or 1 quarter, 4 dimes

At the Fair (page 28)

A. balloon
B. 2 flags
C. ice cream
D. monkey
E. 20 cents
F. 15 cents
G. 3 balloons
H. flag, balloon, ice cream

At the Toy Store (page 29)

A. bear, yo-yo
B. top, drum
C. Sara—top; Kyle—yo-yo
D. Nikki—ball; Brandon—car
E. top and ball; top and yo-yo; ball and yo-yo

Fun with Pennies and Nickels (page 30)

A. The 10 coins should be filled out as follows: 1¢, 5¢, 1¢, 5¢, 1¢, 5¢, 1¢, 5¢, 1¢, 5¢.
Total amount is 30¢.

B. The 10 coins should be filled out as follows: 1¢, 1¢, 5¢, 1¢, 1¢, 5¢, 1¢, 1¢, 5¢, 1¢.
Total amount is 22¢.
Katie has 8 cents more than Bert.

Coin Patterns (page 31)

A. The 10 coins should be filled out as follows: 5¢, 10¢, 5¢, 10¢, 5¢, 10¢, 5¢, 10¢, 5¢, 10¢.
Total amount is 75¢.

B. The 10 coins should be filled out as follows: 5¢, 5¢, 10¢, 5¢, 5¢, 10¢, 5¢, 5¢, 10¢, 5¢.
Total amount is 65¢.

C. The 10 coins should be filled out as follows: 10¢, 5¢, 1¢, 10¢, 5¢, 1¢, 10¢, 5¢, 1¢, 10¢.
Total amount is 58¢.

Find the Fraction (page 32)

A. $^1/_2$
B. $^3/_4$
C. $^3/_6$
D. $^1/_4$
E. $^4/_5$
F. $^1/_3$
G. $^3/_8$
H. $^4/_6$
I. $^2/_4$

Fraction Designs (page 33)

Rectangles should be colored as follows:

A. 1 section red, 2 sections purple
B. 1 section yellow, 5 sections orange
C. 2 sections green, 2 sections yellow
D. 3 sections red, 3 sections yellow
E. 1 section blue, 1 section red, 2 sections yellow
F. 4 sections blue, 1 section purple, 3 sections red

Fruity Halves (page 34)

A. 2 bananas should be colored; $^1/_2$ of 4 = 2
B. 3 oranges should be colored; $^1/_2$ of 6 = 3
C. 5 cherries should be colored; $^1/_2$ of 10 = 5
D. 4 apples should be colored; $^1/_2$ of 8 = 4
E. 1 pineapple should be colored; $^1/_2$ of 2 = 1
F. 6 strawberries should be colored; $^1/_2$ of 12 = 6

Flower Sets (page 35)

A. 3 flowers should be circled.
B. 2 flowers should be circled.
C. 1 flower should be circled.
D. 2 flowers should be circled.
E. 1 flower should be circled.
F. 2 flowers should be circled.
G. 3 flowers should be circled.
H. 4 flowers should be circled.

Toy Car Challenge (page 36)

3 cars are blue, 2 cars are red, and 1 car is yellow.
4 cars would be purple.

Balloon Pairs (page 37)

A. 6
B. 2
C. 12
D. 4
E. 18
F. 8
G. 14
H. 10
I. 20
J. 16

2, 4, 6, 8, 10, 12, 14, 16, 18, 20
The numbers end in 2, 4, 6, 8, and 0. The numbers are the same as when you count by twos.

Draw and Multiply (page 38)

Pictures should be drawn accordingly.

A. 3 × 2 = 6
B. 2 × 5 = 10
C. 5 × 2 = 10
D. 3 × 4 = 12
E. 5 × 3 = 15
F. 2 × 10 = 20
G. 3 × 3 = 9
H. 4 × 4 = 16

Critter Math (page 39)

A. 1 × 6 = 6
B. 3 × 6 = 18
C. 5 × 6 = 30
D. 1 × 3 = 3
E. 2 × 3 = 6
F. 6 × 3 = 18
G. 1 × 8 = 8
H. 2 × 8 = 16
I. 3 × 8 = 24

High-Flying Kites (page 40)

A. 4 × 3 = 12
B. 3 × 6 = 18 (or 6 × 3 = 18)
C. 2 × 7 = 14 (or 7 × 2 = 14)
D. 5 × 6 = 30 (or 6 × 5 = 30)
E. 5 × 4 = 20 (or 4 × 5 = 20)
F. 2 × 8 = 16 (or 8 × 2 = 16)
G. 3 × 7 = 21 (or 7 × 3 = 21)
H. 5 × 8 = 40 (or 8 × 5 = 40)

Missing Shapes (page 41)

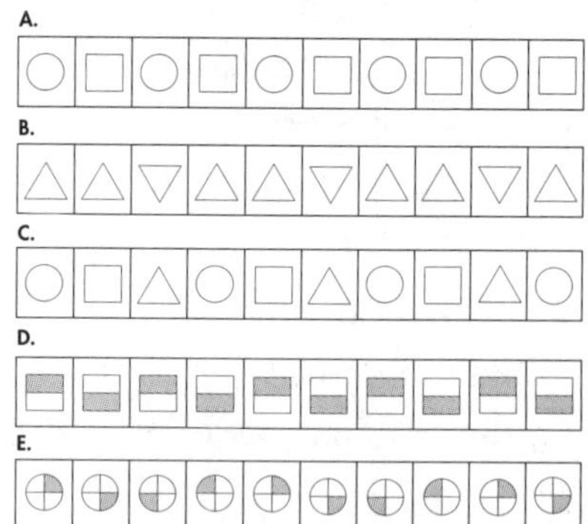

Pretty Beads (page 42)

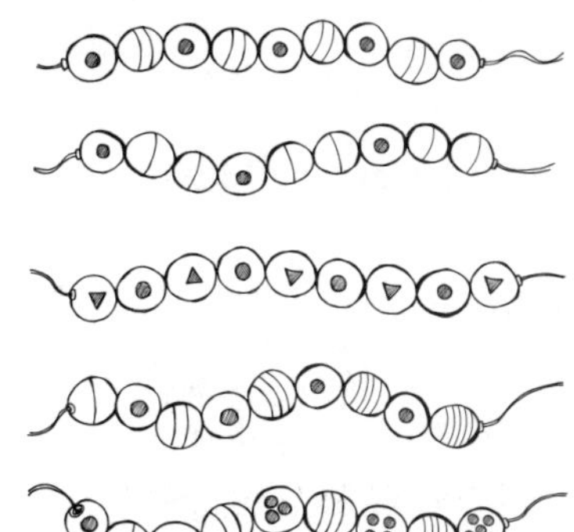

Dot-to-Dots (page 43)

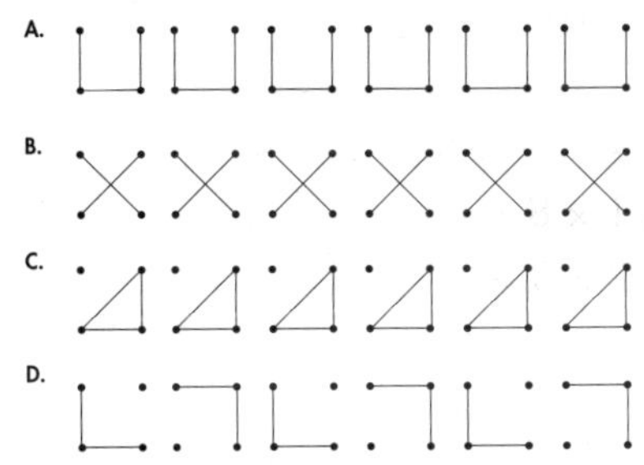

E. Student's patterns will vary.

Dots and Lines (page 44)

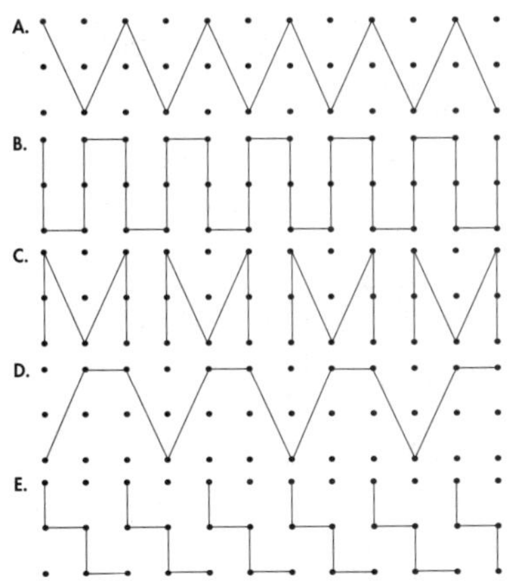

Block Patterns (page 45)

A. 16
B. 25
C. 7
D. 9
E. 10
F. 15

Caterpillar Counting (page 46)

A. 25, 30, 35; add 5
B. 9, 11, 13; add 2
C. 59, 49, 39; subtract 10
D. 20, 24, 28; add 4
E. 11, 16, 22; add 1, add 2, add 3, add 4, and so on

Number Patterns (page 47)

A. 60, 70, 80, 90
B. 66, 77, 88, 99
C. 65, 75, 85, 95
D. 56, 67, 78, 89
E. 1, 6, 1, 7
F. 40, 5, 50, 6
G. 5, 5, 5, 5

Students' patterns will vary.

Dru's Clues (page 48)

A. 50
B. 65
C. 40
D. 14
E. 18
F. 24

Frog Jumps (page 49)

A. 8
B. 6
C. 12, 24

Make Them Equal (page 50)

A. 4
B. 2
C. 2
D. 6
E. 9
F. 2
G. 7
H. 5
I. 3
J. 9

A Balancing Act (page 51)

A. 6
B. 9
C. 7
D. 10
E. 6
F. 3
G. 5
H. 8

Playtime (page 52)

A. 16
B. 14
C. 22
D. 18
E. 12

Snack Time (page 53)

A. 3 red apples, 6 green apples
B. 6 pears, 3 oranges, 3 bananas
C. 2 yellow cookies, 4 green cookies, 6 orange cookies

At the Park (page 54)

A. 18 birds
B. 24 children
C. 12 mothers, 8 fathers
D. 18 children
E. 2 red, 6 yellow, 8 purple

Tip: Students may use various strategies for solving the problems. Some students may wish to use counters, other may want to draw diagrams, and others may prefer to guess and check.

A Three-Horned Fellow (page 55)

A. 6
B. 15
C. 3
D. 18
E. For each triceratops, there are 3 horns; counting by threes.

Looking for Shells (page 56)

A. Chart should be filled out as follows:

	Number of Shells Found Each Time					Total Number
Brad	1	1	1	1	1	5
Joni	2	2	2	2	2	10

Brad found 5 shells. Joni found 10 shells.

B. Chart should be filled out as follows:

	Number of Shells Found Each Time					Total Number
Lynn	2	2	2	2	2	10
Mike	3	3	3	3	3	15

Lynn found 10 shells. Mike found 15 shells.

Math Field Trip (page 57)

A. Chart should be filled out as follows:
Monday 5
Tuesday 7
Wednesday 9
Thursday 11
Friday 13

13 classes visited the zoo on Friday.

B. Chart should be filled out as follows:
Monday 2
Tuesday 4
Wednesday 8
Thursday 16
Friday 32

32 classes visited the museum on Friday.

C. Chart should be filled out as follows:
Monday 10
Tuesday 15
Wednesday 20
Thursday 25
Friday 30

10 classes went to the beach on Monday.

Here Comes the Circus! (page 58)

A. 2 jugglers, 2 bears
B. 4 clowns, 3 elephants
C. 2 lion tamers, 3 lions
D. 4 horses, 4 acrobats

Zoo Clues (page 59)

A. 2 parrots, 2 camels
B. 3 ostriches, 2 hippos
C. 5 ducks, 2 deer
D. 3 peacocks, 4 tigers

Ricky's Rocks (page 60)

round box—6 rocks
square box—8 rocks

Set 2 has more rocks. Set 1 has 20 rocks (6 + 6 + 8) and Set 2 has 22 rocks (8 + 8 + 6).

Who's Who? (page 61)

Boys in order from the shortest to the tallest: Jim, Tom, Sid
Girls in order from the shortest to the tallest: Dee, Sue, Jan, Bev.

A Flower Garden (page 62)

Flowers should be colored as follows: 1 orange, 2 red, 3 yellow.

Colorful Flowers (page 63)

Flowers should be colored as follows: 1 purple, 2 red, 3 blue, 3 yellow.

Bear Buddies (page 64)

Bears should be colored in these pairs: blue and purple, orange and black, brown and yellow.

Tip: It may be helpful for students to manipulate colored squares (blue, purple, orange, black, brown, yellow) in order to solve the problem.

All in the Family (page 65)

A. Jim is 8, Kim is 5.
B. 7
C. Meg is 20, Meg's mom is 40.
D. Cory is 10, Cory's dad is 30, Cory's grandfather is 60.

Sides and Corners (page 66)

A. 3 sides, 3 corners
B. 4 sides, 4 corners
C. 4 sides, 4 corners
D. 6 sides, 6 corners
E. 5 sides, 5 corers
F. 4 sides, 4 corners

Shapes have the same number of corners as they have sides.

Faces and Shapes (page 67)

A.

B. 

C. 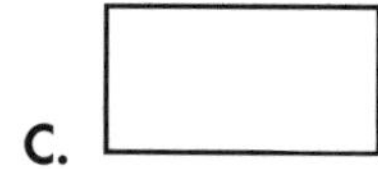

D. 

E. 

F. 

Alike and Different (page 68)

Answers will vary. Possible answers include:

A. Alike: A cube and rectangular prism both have six faces and six corners.
Different: The six faces of a cube are the same size and shape.
A rectangular prism does not have faces that are the same size and shape.

B. Alike: A cylinder and a cone both have faces that are shaped like a circle.
Different: A cylinder has two faces. A cone has only one face.
A cone has a point but a cylinder does not.

C. Alike: A cone and a pyramid both have a point.
Different: A cone has a face that is shaped like a circle, but a pyramid does not.
A cone has curved sides. A pyramid has flat faces.

Sorting Shapes (page 69)

Answers will vary. Possible answers include:

A. The shapes are rectangles. They have four sides.

B. The shapes are triangles. They have three sides.

C. The shapes have no sides. They have curved outlines.

D. The shapes have four sides.

Fishy Squares (page 70)

Fish A—6 squares (5 small squares and 1 large square)

Fish B—4 squares (1 small square, 2 medium squares, and 1 large square)

Fish C—5 squares (3 small squares, 1 medium square, 1 large square)

Tricky Triangles (page 71)

Triangle A—5 triangles (4 small triangles and 1 large triangle)

Triangle B—9 triangles (7 small triangles and 2 large triangles)

Triangle C—13 triangles (9 small triangles, 3 medium triangles, and 1 large triangle)

Shape Designs (page 72)

A. 5
B. 6
C. 4
D. 6

Find the Shape (page 73)

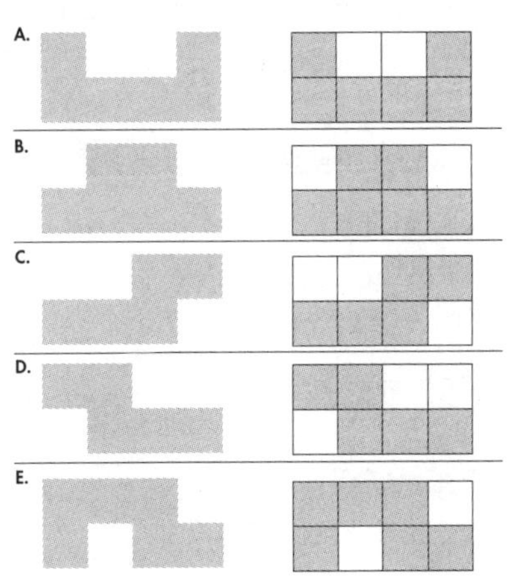

Hide and Seek (page 74)

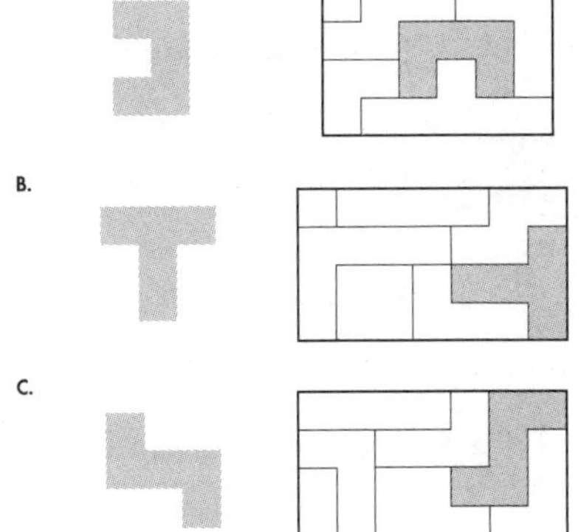

Find the Robot (page 75)

A. 3
B. 2
C. 1
D. 4

Make New Shapes (page 76)

Answers may vary. In some instances, there is more than one possibility. Possible answers include:

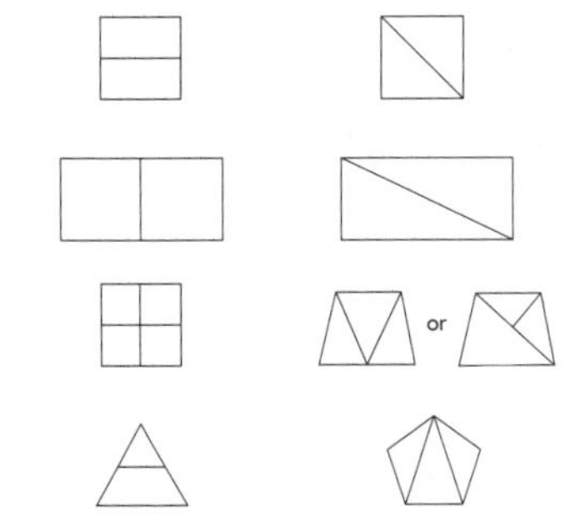

Block Towers (page 77)

A. 8
B. 12
C. 16
D. 12

Tower C used the most blocks.

Fold It in Half (page 78)

A. 2
B. 1
C. 2
D. 2
E. 1
F. 1
G. 2
H. 1

Letter Halves (page 79)

I and H have two lines of symmetry.

Finish the Halves (page 80)

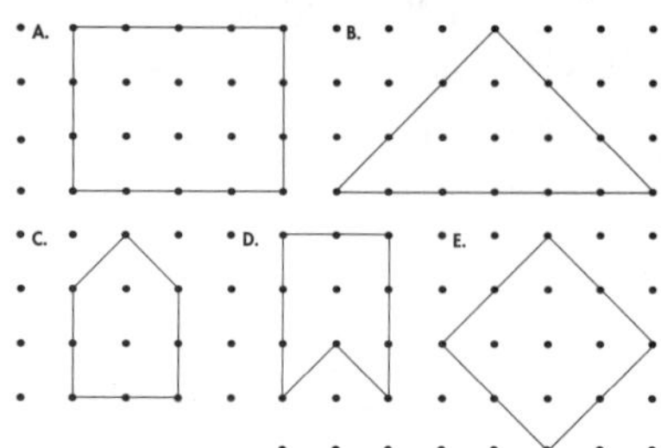

Folded Shapes (page 81)

Divide the Rectangle (page 82)

There are four possibilities:

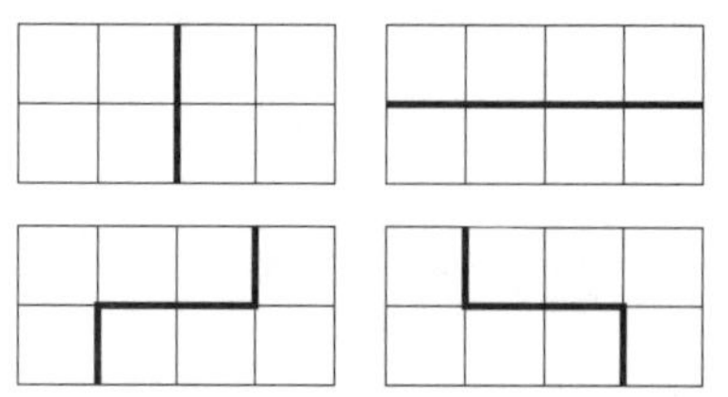

Find the Zoo Animals (page 83)

A. A4
B. F2
C. B1
D. F5
E. B3
F. C4
G. C2
H. E3

On the Farm (page 84)

A. A1
B. B2
C. D2
D. B4
E. C1
F. A3

Answers will vary. Possible answers include:

G. Move 3 spaces to the right. Then move 3 spaces up.
H. Move 2 spaces up and 2 spaces to the right. (Or, move 2 spaces to the right and 2 spaces up.)
I. Move 2 spaces up.

Show the Time (page 85)

Hands on the clocks should be drawn accordingly.

A. 4:00, 5:00, 6:00
B. 9:00, 10:00, 11:00
C. 12:00, 1:00, 2:00
D. 7:30, 8:30, 9:30
E. 11:30, 12:30, 1:30

Ernie's Day (page 86)

Hands on the clock should be drawn accordingly.

A. 8:00
B. 11:30
C. 12:00
D. 5:00
E. 7:30
F. 8:30

Time on the Move (page 87)

Hands on the clock should be drawn accordingly.

A. 1:00, 2:00, 3:00, 4:00, 5:00
B. 4:30, 5:30, 6:30, 7:30, 8:30
C. 10:00, 10:30, 11:00, 11:30, 12:00
D. 2:30, 3:00, 3:30, 4:00, 4:30

Passing Time (page 88)

Hands on the clock should be drawn accordingly

A. 10:15, 11:15, 12:15, 1:15, 2:15
B. 2:45, 3:45, 4:45, 5:45, 6:45
C. 7:15, 7:45, 8:15, 8:45, 9:15
D. 1:45, 2:15, 2:45, 3:15, 3:45

Time Puzzlers (page 89)

A. 2:30
B. 8:15
C. 5:30
D. 9:00
E. 3:00
F. 10:15

Months of the Year (page 90)

A. January
B. May
C. December
D. June
E. February
F. March
G. October
H. April
I. September
J. July
K. November

Calendar Clues (page 91)

A. 31
B. Monday
C. Wednesday
D. Saturday
E. 4
F. October 9
G. Monday, Tuesday, Wednesday

How Much Time? (page 92)

A. Stan
B. Tracey
C. Marcie
D. Tom

To the Bear's Cave (page 93)

A. 4 inches
B. 3 inches
C. 6 inches
D. 7 inches
E. 5 inches

Home Sweet Home (page 94)

A. 6
B. 4
C. 3, 2
D. 2, 3
E. $4^1/_2$

Snaky Lengths (page 95)

A. Mark's snake—10 inches; Sophie's snake—12 inches
B. Kelli's snake—12 inches; Nathan's snake—9 inches
C. Ryan's snake—10 inches; Hannah's snake—20 inches
D. Mel's snake—11 inches; Karen's snake—22 inches

Mice and Cheese (page 96)

A. 6 cm
B. 7 cm
C. 5 cm
D. 8 cm
E. 10 cm
F. 12 cm

On the Go (page 97)

A. 14
B. 15
C. 20
D. 16

C has the longest path; A has the shortest path.

Lighter or Heavier? (page 98)

The following pictures should be circled:

A. pencil
B. book
C. basketball
D. napkin
E. spoon
F. apple

Students' drawings will vary.

What Do They Weigh? (page 99)

The cat is 15 pounds. The dog is 20 pounds.

Students' drawings and answers will vary.

Pints and Cups (page 100)

1 pint	2 pints	3 pints	4 pints	5 pints	6 pints
2 cups	4 cups	6 cups	8 cups	10 cups	12 cups

A. 2 pints
B. 4 pints
C. 6 cups
D. 10 cups
E. 8 cups
F. 6 pints
G. 14 cups

Quarts, Pints, and Cups (page 101)

1 quart	2 quarts	3 quarts	4 pints	5 pints
2 pints	4 pints	6 pints	8 pints	10 pints
4 cups	8 cups	12 cups	16 cups	20 cups

A. 4 pints
B. 8 cups
C. 10 pints
D. 16 cups
E. 3 quarts
F. 4 quarts
G. 12 cups

Fill It Up (page 102)

The following pictures should be circled:

A. 2 pints
B. 1 quart
C. 6 pints
D. 1 gallon
E. 5 quarts
F. 6 cups

Taking Up Space (page 103)

A. 4
B. 7
C. 5
D. 7
E. 8
F. 3
G. E
H. F
I. B, D

Students' drawings will vary.

Floor Tiles (page 104)

A. 12
B. 9
C. 6
D. 14
E. 8
F. 10
G. D
H. C
I. 1
J. 2

Starry Problems (page 105)

	Tally	Number
Stars in the circle only	||	2
Stars in the rectangle only	||||	4
Stars in the triangle only	|	1
Stars in both the triangle and rectangle	|	1
Stars in both the rectangle and circle	|||	3
Total number of stars	𝍸 𝍸 |	11

Hunting for Bones (page 106)

	Tally	Number
Bones in the small circle only	||	2
Bones in the large circle only	||||	4
Bones in both the large circle and the small circle	|	1
Bones not in a circle	|||	3
Total number of bones	卌 卌	10

Sorting Shapes (page 107)

A. The shapes are all triangles.
B. The shapes are shaded.
C. The shapes are triangles that are shaded.
D. A picture of a shaded triangle should be drawn.

Under the Sea (page 108)

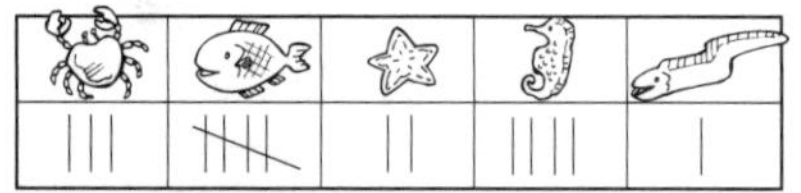

A. 3
B. 5
C. 2
D. 3
E. 15

Favorite Pets (page 109)

A. 6
B. 5
C. dog
D. fish
E. cats
F. 25

Baby Bunnies (page 110)

Bert
Kris
Mike
Pam
Jake
1 2 3 4 5 6 7

A. Pam
B. Jake
C. Mike
D. Kris
E. 18

Favorite Places (page 111)

Zoo
Park
Library
Museum
1 2 3 4 5 6 7 8 9

The park got the most votes. The museum got the least votes.

How Tall? (page 112)

A. 15 inches
B. Denny's plant
C. Benny's plant
D. Jenny's plant and Penny's plant
E. Kenny's plant

A Juicy Graph (page 113)

A. 4
B. 3
C. apple juice
D. grape juice
E. 7
F. 10
G. 20

Butterfly Hunt (page 114)

A. 6
B. 12
C. 10
D. 4
E. 2
F. 28

Pick a Cube (page 115)

A. purple; There are more purple cubes than any other color.
B. yellow; There is only one yellow cube.
C. Get three cubes—one purple, one orange, and one yellow. Since there is only one of each color, all three colors have an equal chance of being picked.

Andy's Socks (page 116)

A. less likely
B. more likely
C. yellow sock
D. red
E. yellow

A Flag Maker (page 117)

Flags should be colored to show these combinations: blue flag with red star, blue flag with yellow star, purple flag with red star, purple flag with yellow star, green flag with red star, green flag with yellow star.

Pairs of Fish (page 118)

Fish should be colored to show these combinations: red and red, red and yellow, red and orange, yellow and yellow, yellow and orange, orange and orange.

Mr. Drake's Ducks (page 119)

Ducks should be colored as follows: yellow duck with red bow, yellow duck with purple bow, yellow duck with blue bow, orange duck with red bow, orange duck with purple bow, orange duck with blue bow, brown duck with red bow, brown duck with purple bow, brown duck with blue bow.